CREMATION
OR
BURIAL?

CREMATION OR BURIAL?
A Jewish View

DORON KORNBLUTH

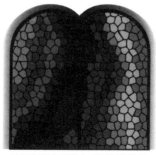

MOSAICA PRESS

Also by Doron Kornbluth:
Raising Kids to LOVE Being Jewish (Mosaica Press, 2009)
Why Be Jewish? (Mosaica Press, 2011)

Mosaica Press, Inc.

© 2012 by Doron Kornbluth

Typeset by Rayzel Broyde

All rights reserved

ISBN 978-1-937887-01-8

No part of this publication may be translated, reproduced, stored in a retrieval system, or transmitted in any form or by any means, electronic, mechanical, photocopying, recording, or otherwise, without prior permission in writing from both the copyright holder and the publisher.

Published and distributed by:

Mosaica Press, Inc.
Jerusalem/Monsey
www.mosaicapress.com
info@mosaicapress.com

Printed in Israel

JewishDeathAndMourning.org

is proud to dedicate this book to
the many Jews throughout history
who were denied a proper Jewish burial.

May their souls be elevated in Heaven.

Special thanks to the

Siegel Family

of Deerfield, Illinois

and the

Horowitz Family

of Los Angeles, California

whose early moral and material support made the research and development of this work possible.

O Man,
Whoever you are and from wherever you come
(for I know that you will come)
I am Cyrus,
and I won for the Persians their empire.
Do not, therefore, begrudge me
This little earth that covers my body.

— Epitaph of Cyrus the Great
(d. 529 BCE)

Show me the manner in which a nation cares for its dead,
and I will measure with mathematical exactness
the tender mercies of its people,
their respect for the laws of the land
and their loyalty to high ideals.

— William Gladstone,
British Prime Minister
(1809–1898)

Contents

Foreword 11
Acknowledgments 15
Introduction 17

Part 1: Understanding Burial and Cremation

1. Monotheism and Burial 25
2. The Army and the Torah Scroll 31
3. Judaism, Burial, and Cremation 35
4. Desiderata 41
5. Feelings 47
6. Symbolism and Meaning of Burial and Cremation .. 51
7. Graves Are for the Living 59

Part 2: Practicalities

8. The Process of Cremation 73
9. Mobility 83
10. Scandals and More 89

  11. Cost Factors 93

Part 3: Environmental Concerns
  12. Land Is for the Living 107
  13. Energy Use 115
  14. Toxic Emissions 123
  15. Giving Back to Planet Earth 133

Part 4: Spiritual Concerns
  16. The Soul Is Aware 143
  17. Rational View of Resurrection 147

  Conclusion 157

Appendix A:
  An Introduction to Jewish Burial Customs 161
Appendix B:
  An Introduction to Jewish Mourning Customs 165
Appendix C:
  Cremation in Israel? 171

  Selected Bibliography 175
  About the Author 180
  Dear Dad 187
  Dear Son 189

Foreword

Many years ago, my father's sister died suddenly. When I asked my father if I could go to the funeral, he said no — there wouldn't be one. Instead, her ashes were scattered in the Pacific Ocean, as she had requested.

Like all my relatives, I grew up without much Jewish knowledge. I didn't know what a Jewish burial was supposed to be, and knew even less about cremation. Yet somehow I felt unsettled — especially when my father mentioned that he might request the same thing. While I couldn't explain my uneasiness, something just didn't sit right.

Another aunt, my mother's sister, had had a hard life. She suffered as a child and, despite having a wonderful marriage for nearly fifty years, struggled many years to raise a special-needs child. Last year, she became ill and confided in me her plans for cremation. I knew I wanted to convince her otherwise. I looked for a book and researched online. Unfortunately, I could not find anything that would be meaningful to her personally, as all I found seemed either too religious or too commercial. In any event, what I shared did not really speak to her.

My aunt was very sensitive to the environment. While she never researched the subject, I believe she felt (erroneously) that cremation was a better eco-choice than burial. She was cremated and her ashes were strewn across the Californian Redwood forest. To this day, many of her relatives are saddened that we will never be able to visit her place of rest. She died shortly before this book was finished, and I'll always wonder if things would have been different if I had been able to give her a copy.

Around the same time, another relative of mine passed away. My eighty-year-old uncle died alone in his trailer. A broken man financially, his final words to his grandsons were to be "good boys." While he sensed it wasn't the Jewish way, my uncle knew little of Judaism, and he had indicated to his children that his body should be cremated in order to save money. His children were not happy about the prospect, but followed his wishes and sent the body to the crematorium.

When they realized that the process was neither quick nor clean, they felt uneasy. When they were told that the crematorium intended to cut out his hip and pacemaker so as not to damage the cremation equipment, the family was shocked and distraught. None of them wanted to do a cremation. They knew it wasn't the Jewish way, but didn't know what to do. For more than two weeks his body lay in the cold crematorium.

This time, I realized that I needed to get involved. I knew from experience that cremations can leave families empty, angry, and with a lack of closure. I prayed that the cremation shouldn't happen. I called JewishDeathAndMourning.org and sponsored Mishnah study in his merit. I talked with my cousins, and explained the benefits of a Jewish burial.

With a little guidance and a little financial help, my cousins decided to give their father a Jewish burial. His body was carefully brought to a Jewish funeral home. A guardian (*shomer*) was assigned to pray and watch over him until burial. A sense of peace pervaded the family. My uncle was lovingly buried. A month later, a headstone was put up. Various members of the family go to visit his resting place from time to time. They often express to me how happy they are with their decision. He is at peace — and so are they.

Only one generation ago, cremation was unknown in the Jewish community. Today, over one third of Jews across America are choosing it. This decision is almost always due to a lack of information. Written with understanding, respect, and a wealth of research, the book in your hands points out common misconceptions about cremation and beautifully explains *why* burial is so important. It gives readers a whole new perspective on this ultimate question.

I urge you to read every page carefully.

—Robin Davina Meyerson

Acknowledgments

Researching, writing, editing, and preparing this book for publication took over two years. I received much help. Rabbi Elchonon Zohn, foremost authority on burial issues in the United States and the head of the Chevra Kadisha of Queens, New York, kindly shared his valuable time and expertise. Rabbi Dov Lev and Rabbi Menashe Bleiweiss, talented writers as well as Torah scholars, edited and made numerous improvements. Rabbi Naftali Silverberg, Rabbi Dovid Kentridge, and Rabbi Arnie Gluck shared many insights, as did a broad spectrum of Jewish educators. Rabbi Yaacov Haber deserves special mention for significantly improving the book in many ways. Any mistakes or omissions are my responsibility alone.

The staff of Mosaica Press took a manuscript and turned it into a beautiful book. Special thanks to Mrs. Chaya Baila Gavant for her professional copyediting and proofreading, and to Mrs. Rayzel Broyde and Mrs. Chani Leiser for their excellent design. I am delighted to publish with Mosaica Press and hope to do so for many years to come.

Many thanks to Mrs. Robin Davina Meyerson, whose devotion to spreading the word about the importance of kosher Jewish burial and mourning practices is inspiring. Without her tireless efforts, the publication of this work would have been seriously delayed. Her suggestions for improving the work were also of great help.

I am glad to give a special thanks to Rabbi Moshe Haikins and his organization, JewishDeathAndMourning.org, for sponsoring the publication of this book as well as its accompanying educational videos (to be available on their site as they are produced). Rabbi Haikins adopted this project as his own, and invested time and money to help get the message out. The mission of JewishDeathAndMourning.org is to help Jews of all backgrounds provide Kaddish, Mishnah study, and other traditional remembrances for their deceased loved ones. I am delighted to have them as a partner.

Many friends and students helped and encouraged me. My doronkornbluth.com e-newsletter article on cremation generated more response than almost any other article in recent years. I appreciate my readers' kind words and comments on this sensitive issue.

Deep thanks to my parents, whose support has never faltered, and whose pride in my writing and teaching makes me, in turn, proud. And much love to Zachariah, Mattisyahu, Simcha, Binah, Hillel, and Rachel, who bring light and laughter into my life. My in-laws, Jack and Joy Siegel, offered support, love, encouragement, and many helpful corrections. I am in their debt.

To my wife: Your devotion keeps me going. My preoccupation with cremation may not have made me the most upbeat of companions recently, but your belief in the importance of this project helped bring about its timely completion.

Doron Kornbluth
October 2011

Introduction

Today, a large and increasing number of people in Western countries are choosing cremation for themselves and for their deceased loved ones. What is the cause of cremation's increasing popularity? Consider these explanations:

1. Financial concerns: Cremation seems — and often is — cheaper than burial.

2. Environmental concerns: Burial seems to waste land and pollute the environment. Also, scattering seems like a beautiful eco-friendly alternative.

3. Mobility concerns: Since children and grandchildren move from city to city, visiting gravesites has become more of a burden than ever. Isn't it easier to "take Grandma along" or simply scatter the remains into the ocean? Why make the kids feel guilty about not visiting?

4. Discomfort with decomposition: Who wants to decompose underground? Cremation seems quicker and cleaner.

5. Distance from tradition: Burial was always the traditional thing to do. Recent history has seen less traditional generations. By definition, people who are less traditional do fewer traditional things.

Furthermore, in 1963, author Jessica Mitford released her bestselling *The American Way of Death,* which exposed what she considered to be "extravagances" and "dishonesty" within the US funeral industry. While her accusations were largely unfair, the industry has never fully recovered from this critique. Who wants a used-car salesman to bury Dad?

In many people's modern consciousness, it seems, cremation and burial are viewed as opposites. Cremation represents the world of nature, trendy eco-consciousness, fiscal responsibility, simplicity, and Eastern-style spirituality. Traditional burial represents the world of pretension, pollution, conspicuous consumption, and organized religion.

As one author put it,

> Cremation ... [has] become a matter of style. Cremationists associated the embalming and burial regime with the fake and the artificial, and aligned cremation with authenticity and naturalness.[1]

With this background in mind, it is therefore quite understandable why many intelligent and well-intentioned people today are choosing cremation.

Why is it, then, that many people are uncomfortable with cremation? And why are many Jews, in particular, against cremation? Is there another side to the story?

As we will see, the aforementioned assumptions about cremation are largely unfounded. For example, cremation is *not* better for the

---

1 Stephen Prothero, *Purified by Fire: A History of Cremation in America* (Berkeley, CA: University of California Press, 2001), 183.

environment, *does not* resolve mobility problems, and is often *not* significantly cheaper. Furthermore, when one looks into it, there are many important and meaningful reasons to choose burial. In arguing on behalf of traditional burial, we should note that

> whether to bury or to burn is … no trivial matter. It touches on issues as important as perceptions of the self, attitudes toward the body, views of history, styles of ritual, and beliefs in God and the afterlife.[2]

Throughout history, societies have adopted varying approaches to dealing with corpses. Some have buried them in the ground and some have cremated them. Others sealed them away in elaborate mausoleums with food and drink, mummified them, left them for the vultures, seated them in a corner of the dining room, cannibalized them, set them adrift, boiled them, and done the unthinkable to the bodies of their loved ones. Presumably, most people simply followed their neighbors' example in deciding what method to use for the disposal of human remains.

Today, mirroring the developments in Western society, at least 30 percent of Jewish deaths in North America and Europe are followed by cremations,[3] and the percentage is on the rise.

Cremation is so common that it is becoming the norm in certain communities. So, if you have chosen to cremate the body of a loved one, don't get caught up in guilt — it is happening all around us. Until now, little information has been available on the subject from a contemporary Jewish view. Good Jewish people are making this choice like most Americans do — in moments of grief, and without much information available.

That being said, the new cremation fad is a significant change from Jewish history and philosophy. Jews have been making this

---

2 Prothero, *Purified by Fire*, 5.
3 Estimated by Rabbi Elchonon Zohn of the Chevra Kadisha of Queens, New York, and founder and director of the National Association of Chevra Kadisha.

"last decision" for millennia in a deliberate and meaningful way, and have opted for burial because of its profound moral, historical, and spiritual ramifications. Burial is the right choice for Jews, past, present, and future.

This book will begin to explore both ancient and modern explanations for choosing burial, including both the mystical and the rational, as well as articulate the underlying beauty behind the practice.

Part 1
Understanding Burial and Cremation

Introduction to Part 1

"Jews don't do that" may have been enough for previous generations to continue the practices of their ancestors, but not anymore. With the increase in the number of cremations across the West, people need to know *why* burial is the method of choice for Jews today.

In this first section of the book, we will focus on the meaning and symbolism of burial and cremation. Which groups of people are buried and which cremated? Why? We will explain what burial and cremation teach the living, and what effects each one has on society.

We will also explore Judaism's connection to burial, and gain insight and inspiration from the thought-provoking choices regularly made by the State of Israel and the Israel Defense Forces (IDF).

-1-
Monotheism and Burial

Cremation is not a new idea. Many ancient societies burned bodies. Thousands of cremated remains have been found in Native American, Australian indigenous, Scandinavian, Tibetan, and ancient Greek and Roman archeological sites, and the practice eventually spread into Western Europe as well. Eastern religions such as Hinduism, Jainism, and Buddhism often require the practice, and in most cases have done so for thousands of years.[4]

While cremation was well-known in the ancient pagan (polytheistic) world, it was never universal. Jewish law and tradition have always prohibited cremation. So does Islam, the Eastern Orthodox Church, many evangelical groups, and various other Christian sects. The Catholic Church banned cremation for over fifteen hundred years,[5] effectively eliminating it in Christian lands.

Best-selling author and talk-show commentator Professor Stephen Prothero's oft-cited book, *Purified by Fire: A History of*

---

4 *Wikipedia*, s.v. "Cremation," http://en.wikipedia.org/wiki/Cremation.
5 The ban took real force when Christian King Charlemagne outlawed cremation in 780 CE.

Cremation in America, shows in great detail how cremation's popularity declined with the spread of Christianity. In essence, wherever monotheism went, cremation disappeared. If one maps out the percentage of cremations practiced today and throughout history, what appears — incredibly — is an accurate map of monotheistic belief. Cremation is far more common in polytheistic, secularized,[6] and "post-Christian" regions and cultures. Cremation accounts for over 90 percent of burial choices in Japan and India, and over 70 percent in heavily secularized Switzerland and Great Britain. In parts of the world inhabited by Jews, Muslims, and Orthodox Christians (as well as other Christian denominations), for instance, cremation rates are far lower.

Burial and the Bible

The (Hebrew) Bible is the first and most basic textual source for monotheism. Every reference to the subject in the Bible commands or encourages burial and shows disfavor to cremation. The Bible is consistent on the subject, and examples abound.

Abraham was buried:

> Then Abraham ... died in a good old age ... and his sons Isaac and Ishmael buried him in the cave of Machpelah ...[7]

Sarah was buried:

> And Sarah died in Kiryat-Arba ... And Abraham came to mourn for Sarah, and to weep for her. And

---

6 "It is rather obvious that the dramatic increases in American cremation rates (from 0.003 percent in 1900 to 27.25 percent in 2001) are directly related to the growing impact that secularism has had, and continues to have, on Americans ... especially since the 1960's" (Alvin Schmidt, *Dust to Dust or Ashes to Ashes? A Biblical and Christian Examination of Cremation* [Salisbury, MA: Regina Orthodox Press, 2005], 108).

7 Genesis 25:8–10.

Abraham stood up from before his dead, and spoke to the children of Heth, saying, "I am a stranger and a sojourner with you: give me a possession of a burying place with you, that I may bury my dead …"[8]

Rachel was buried:

And Rachel died, and was buried on the way to Efrat … Jacob set up a monument upon her grave: that is the monument that is on Rachel's grave until today.[9]

Isaac was buried:

And Isaac … died … being old and in the fullness of years; and his sons Esau and Jacob buried him.[10]

Jacob was buried:

And when Jacob finished instructing his children … he died … and his sons carried him into the land of Canaan, and buried him in the cave of the field of Machpelah …[11]

Joshua was buried:

And it came to pass … that Joshua … the servant of God, died … and they buried him …[12]

Elazar the High Priest was buried:

And Elazar the son of Aaron died; and they buried him on a hill that was owned by Pinchas …[13]

---

8 Ibid. 23:2–4.
9 Ibid. 35:19–20.
10 Ibid., 29.
11 Ibid. 49:33, 50:4–13.
12 Joshua 24:29–30.
13 Ibid., 33.

Samuel the Prophet was buried:

> And Samuel died; and all the Israelites gathered together, and eulogized him, and buried him …[14]

King David was buried:

> So David lay to rest with his ancestors, and was buried in the city of David.[15]

God's Choice

Many more examples exist, but perhaps one of the most powerful testaments to the importance of burial is the fact that God Himself chose to bury Moses:

> So Moses, the servant of God, died there in the land of Moab … And He [God] buried him in a valley in the land of Moab …but no one knows his burial place, to this day.[16]

In "disposing" of the body of Moses, God had endless options. He could have used fire to cremate. He could have sent vultures to tear off the flesh like in Zoroastrian and Tibetan sky burials. He could have scattered Moses's remains in the Red Sea (a.k.a. the Sea of Reeds), the scene of Moses's greatest hour. God didn't choose those methods. Even though no one would ever visit the grave (God kept the location hidden to prevent it from being used for idol worship), burial was then and remains now — literally — God's choice.

Until recently, throughout history, it was obvious to all that monotheists practiced burial. Both those who believed in one God

---

[14] 1 Samuel 25:1.
[15] 1 Kings 2:10.
[16] Deuteronomy 34:5–6.

(monotheists) and those who didn't (pagans and atheists) recognized the wide divergence of burial practices. Throughout history, Jews knew of alternative methods of disposition, and rejected them.

The historic development of burial choices is remarkable. In general, burial followed the belief in one God and cremation followed the belief in multiple gods, or the weakening of belief in any god.

What is the philosophical connection between belief in one God and burial?

We'll return to this question later on in the book. What do you think?

-2-
The Army and the Torah Scroll

On July 16, 2008, in the presence of Red Cross and UN observers, the State of Israel transferred to the Hezbollah terrorist organization four jailed Hezbollah fighters, about two hundred other Lebanese and Palestinian militants captured in various wars and anti-terrorist operations, and PLFP member Samir Kuntar, who was convicted of brutally murdering a father and his four-year-old daughter.

Israel let these 205 terrorists go free. What did Israel receive in return?

Israel received, in total, the remains of two Israeli soldiers, Ehud Goldwasser and Eldad Regev, captured in 2006.

The State of Israel has made many lopsided exchanges with its enemies. For example, in November 1983, Israel traded 4,600 Arab prisoners for six Israeli soldiers.

What is most startling in the 2008 exchange was that Israel gave up *live* enemies in order to retrieve the *dead* bodies of its soldiers.

This was not the first time it happened: In 1990, Israel released fifty-one prisoners in return for proof of a missing Israeli soldier's death. In 2004, Israel gave up 436 Arab prisoners and the bodies of 59 Lebanese militants in exchange for one (live) Israeli civilian and the bodies of three Israeli soldiers.[17]

Whether or not to conduct such exchanges is a complicated question, and not one we can adequately deal with here. What is of interest to us is that, virtually alone in the world, and with the backing of a strong majority of its population, Israel *actually does it*. Providing a proper Jewish burial for its soldiers is ingrained in Israel's conscience. Let us try to understand why.

Rescuing Torah Scrolls

Many Americans first heard of the holiness of Torah scrolls when ZAKA Rescue and Recovery, helped by units of the US National Guard, rode in inflatable rafts to reach New Orleans's Beth Israel Synagogue to salvage its Torah scrolls from Hurricane Katrina in 2005.[18] Today, rabbis and congregations around the world try to locate and save Torah scrolls that were damaged in the Iraq War, buried or desecrated in the Holocaust, or stolen by the Communists. Jews are willing to pay exorbitant prices, and sometimes take great risks, for the sake of a Torah scroll.

When found, these ancient Torah scrolls are inevitably damaged. Sometimes they can be repaired by a scribe. When repair is impossible, the Torah scrolls are buried: a dignified "end" to the "life" of the Torah scroll.

Our tradition explains that once parchment is used for a holy purpose — to hold the letters of the Torah — the scroll retains that

---

17 Dan Balilty, "Israel's Agonizing Debate over Prisoner Swaps," *CBC News*, July 16, 2008, http://www.cbc.ca/world/story/2008/07/09/f-prisoner-swaps.html.
18 Congregation Beth Israel, "Beth Israel and Hurricane Katrina," http://bethisraelnola.com/beth-israel-and-hurricane-katrina/.

holiness forever. Even if severely damaged and no longer kosher, the scroll is still holy and must be buried honorably. Torah scrolls are very important. And they retain their holiness even once desecrated or damaged beyond repair.

People are more important than Torah scrolls — in the face of danger, saving a person takes clear precedence over saving a scroll. Human beings contain a spark of holiness — and human bodies retain their honor, dignity, and holiness even when the soul has left.

Jewish sources explicitly make the connection between a human body and a Torah scroll.

> Anyone dealing with a dead body must know that he is dealing with a sacred object: The body of a person is not simply a container for holiness, that served the holy soul, rather it itself became sacred ... similar to a Torah scroll.[19]

> During the life of a person, while his soul ... is in it, [the body] is called a living Torah scroll (it is important a person not forget this, and be careful with his Torah scroll and those of his friends), and so, one who witnesses the moment of death of a person it is as if he is watching a Torah scroll burn ...[20]

A living person contains holiness. Like a Torah scroll. And a dead body retains its holiness, like an old and damaged Torah scroll.

Because of its great holiness, a dead body is to be treated with great reverence. Jewish funeral practices are based on the overriding principle of the sanctity of the human body. The body is never left alone[21] because doing so would be like abandoning it — "like an object that one no longer wants, sitting in disgrace."[22] The

---

19 Rabbi Yechiel Michel Tucazinsky, *Gesher HaChaim*, 1:64.
20 Talmud, Tractate *Moed Katan* 25a, and Tucazinsky, *Gesher HaChaim*, 1:65.
21 Even when there is no real danger of something happening to it.
22 Ibid., 65–66.

body is reverentially cleansed by trained and caring members of the honored Jewish burial society, the *chevra kadisha* (literally, the "holy society"). The entire burial process is done with the utmost respect and decorum.

Surprisingly, Judaism teaches that our bodies don't actually belong to us. They belong to God and are on loan to us (the real "us" being our souls) so that we can function in the world. We are our bodies' custodians, not their owners, and should not destroy something that is not ours.

Furthermore, our bodies don't only *belong* to God — they actually *resemble* God. The Torah says that humans were created *betzelem Elokim*, "in God's image."[23] Since God is incorporeal — has no body or physical limitations of any kind — Jewish commentators understand the verse to refer to us being God-like in our ability to think, choose, act morally, and rise above the physical.

Yet our *physical* bodies are understood to be God-like as well. They give us the ability to create and to help others. We are able to lead dignified[24] and refined lives, with at least a small part of the "dignity" of God. In these ways and others, our bodies "resemble" God.

Bodies of the deceased are also the last remnant of what was, just recently, a loving and beloved human being. As one undertaker put it:

> The bodies of our newly dead are not debris, nor remnant ... They are, rather, changelings, incubates, hatchlings of a new reality that bear our names and dates, our image and likenesses, as surely in the eyes and ears of our children and grandchildren as did word of our birth in the ears of our parents and their parents. It is wise to treat such new things tenderly, carefully, with honor.[25]

---

23 Genesis 1:27.
24 Notice that we stand upright, unlike animals.
25 Thomas Lynch, *The Undertaking: Life Studies from the Dismal Trade* (New York: W. W. Norton & Company, 1997), 22.

-3-
Judaism, Burial, and Cremation

Roughly two thousand years ago, Roman historian Tacitus wrote that "the Jews bury rather than burn their dead."[26]

He was right. Aside from the many examples we've seen, there is a direct commandment to bury the dead:

Deuteronomy 21:23 discusses the case of an evil criminal who is put to death. Even in that extreme case, the command is given, "You shall surely bury him," teaching a general principle for all cases. The obligation to bury is so strong that even the high priest — who zealously avoided all contact with all forms of death — must personally give the dead a proper burial if no one else can do so.[27]

---

26 Tacitus, *Histories* 5:5.
27 Burial in the Bible was chosen even when it was a more difficult choice. Joseph was sold into slavery and rose up to be prime minister of Egypt: "Joseph said to his brothers: 'I am dying, and God will surely remember you, and take you from this land into the land which He swore to Abraham, to Isaac, and to Jacob.' Joseph bound the Israelites by an oath, 'God will surely remember you, and you will take my bones from here' " (Genesis 50:24–25).

The Talmud,[28] Maimonides,[29] and the Code of Jewish Law[30] all codify the commandment to bury the dead.

The Importance of Burial

Proper Jewish burial is so important that even if someone requests not to be buried, or his heirs do not desire to bury him, the body still needs to be buried. Lack of burial (whether through cremation or any other method of disposal) is considered a disgrace to the deceased, humanity, and God.[31] Jewish tradition[32] is clear that cremation is a severe prohibition, and is, in fact, the antithesis of the aforementioned commandment[33] and a direct transgression of Judaism.

When the Jews left Egypt, the promise made to Joseph was not forgotten: "Moses took the bones of Joseph with him for he [Joseph] had bound the Israelites by an oath: 'When God remembers you, you must take my bones from here' " (Exodus 13:19).

When the Jews entered the Promised Land, they finally fulfilled their oath: "And the bones of Joseph, which the Israelites brought up out of Egypt, they buried in Shechem, in a plot that Jacob bought from the sons of Hamor ... for a hundred pieces of silver ..." (Joshua 24:32).

Cremation was not unknown then. In fact, it was widely practiced in some parts of the ancient world. If Joseph wanted his remains to be in Israel, it would have been much easier to cremate them and take the urn along. But this was not an option for biblical figures: death required burial.

28   *Sanhedrin* 46b.
29   *Sefer Ha-Mitzvot* 231, 536; *Laws of Mourning*, ch. 12.
30   *Yoreh Dei'ah* 362.
31   As Rabbi Naftali Silverberg puts it, "If someone requests to be cremated or buried in a manner which is not in accordance with Jewish tradition, we nevertheless provide him/her with a Jewish burial. It is believed that since the soul has now arrived to the World of Truth it surely sees the value of a proper Jewish burial, and thus administering a traditional Jewish burial is actually granting what the person truly wishes at the moment. Furthermore, if anyone, all the more so your father and mother, asks you to damage or hurt their body, you are not allowed to do so. For our bodies do not belong to us, they belong to God" (Rabbi Naftali Silverberg, "Why Does Jewish Law Forbid Cremation?" Chabad.org, http://www.chabad.org/library/article_cdo/aid/510874/jewish/Why-does-Jewish-law-forbid-cremation.htm).
32   Tractate *Sanhedrin* 46b and other sources mentioned here.
33   Rabbi Silverberg: "The Jerusalem Talmud (*Nazir* 7:1) explains that this requires us to bury the body in its entirety, not after it has been diminished through cremation or

Jewish tradition rejects cremation so unambiguously that, as a deterrent measure, cremated remains were historically not allowed in Jewish cemeteries.[34] In a similar vein, traditionally, one of the first things a new Jewish community does is set up a cemetery and burial society — making sure that proper Jewish burial is available to all.

Rabbi David Begoun[35] offers several illustrations of the fact that burying the dead is *really* important to Judaism:

- Rabbi Ephraim Oshry was rabbi of the Kovno Ghetto during the Holocaust, answering thousands of questions from Jews of all backgrounds. After the war, he published much of this correspondence in a five-volume compendium entitled *Questions and Answers from the Depths*.[36] A Jew secretly asked[37] the following question: To survive, he had disguised himself as a German. No one knew that he was a Jew. This hidden Jew was dying of cancer and would be buried in a Christian cemetery with a cross over his body, surrounded by Nazis. He asked, "Perhaps I should be cremated to avoid this?" Rabbi Oshry answered: Absolutely not! Jews *must* do all they can to avoid cremation. He mentions that in ancient times the bodies of many rabbis were transported from Babylonia to Israel, while it would have been much easier to cremate the bodies first, and lists many numerous

---

in any other manner: 'You must bury him in entirety, not partially. From this verse we extrapolate that the command was not fulfilled if the person was partially buried.' Cremating a body destroys most of the body, making burial of the flesh impossible, and thus violates the biblical command" (Silverberg, "Why Forbid Cremation?").

34 *Melamed L'ho'il* 2:114. Also, many of the laws of mourning are not to be observed for someone who deliberately chose cremation.
35 Rabbi David Begoun, "Journey of the Soul: Cremation versus Burial," http://www.judaismwithoutwalls.org/audio.htm.
36 In Hebrew, *She'eilos U'Teshuvos MiMa'amakim*.
37 *She'eilos U'Teshuvos MiMa'amakim* 3:3.

sources backing his decision.

- The Torah discusses complex concepts in only a few words, being very succinct, yet emphasizes burial repeatedly. Far from being silent on burial, our tradition seems to *overemphasize* it: evidently, this idea is important.

- The commandment to bury is not really one commandment but two — a positive commandment to bury and a negative commandment not to *not* bury. Why the double commandment? To emphasize its importance.

The Holocaust

Memories of the Holocaust have prevented many Jews from choosing cremation. As these memories fade, cremation rates have risen.

Yet, as we will see, the Holocaust was never the main reason, or even one of the main reasons, that Jews avoid cremation. That being said, it bears noting that burning has historically been a primary means of eliminating Jews (Nimrod's attempt to kill Abraham, the Inquisition, and the Holocaust are only a few examples). After they were murdered, the bodies were cremated, essentially declaring, "You no longer exist. Nothing from you exists. Your people will soon not exist and there will be no memory of them …"

When Jews choose burial today, they are identifying with — and strengthening — the historic Jewish insistence on burial. Burial declares that not only was the extermination of the Jews monstrous, but that the burning of their bodies was also a terrible crime. Against their will, millions of Jews were robbed of proper Jewish burial, and the world was robbed of the chance to properly commemorate their lives.

The Jewish Choice

Cremation rates among Jews today might be much lower if people were aware of how important burial is to Judaism. Cremation has existed as an option for thousands of years — and yet both Jews and Judaism rejected it, generation after generation.

Society's views on burial and cremation have changed several times and no doubt will change again. Fads come and fads go. The Jewish view hasn't changed: In an ancient world in which criminals were mutilated and left to the dogs, Judaism said that every human being is created in the image of God — and must be respectfully buried.[38]

In this final choice, by opting for burial, we align ourselves with our tradition and stand firm with the many millions of Jews throughout history who insisted on proper Jewish burials for themselves and their loved ones.

---

[38] While this work is focused on Jews, note that most sources seem to indicate that burial is preferable for non-Jews as well.

-4-

Desiderata

In the 1920s, an American lawyer named Max Ehrmann wrote a poem called "Desiderata" that later became famous. Among its most memorable lines are the following:

> You are a child of the universe,
> no less than the trees and the stars;
> You have a right to be here.
> And whether or not it is clear to you,
> No doubt the universe is unfolding as it should.

In 1972, the *National Lampoon* published Tony Hendra's parody of the above, which he called "Deteriorata" —

> You are a fluke of the universe.
> You have no right to be here.
> Whether you can hear it or not,
> The universe is laughing behind your back.

Which is it?
Are we, as individuals, important?
Does each one of us count?
Do our lives matter?

The 1970s rock band Kansas answered decisively, if a bit melodramatically, when they sang:

> All we do
> Crumbles to the ground …
> Nothin' lasts forever
> but the earth and sky
> It slips away …
>
> Dust in the wind
> All we are is dust in the wind …
> Dust in the wind …
> Dust in the wind …

Dehumanization

Most of us know the basic facts of the Holocaust. The Nazis hated many people, but they reserved a special hatred for the Jews, who were targeted for complete destruction. Nazi propagandists made films interspersing images of Jews with rats. Their literature described the Jews not as individuals, but as an amorphous group that constantly plots to destroy the world. Jews were shipped en masse to extermination camps, where they were stripped, shaved, and in some locations had numbers branded into their arms to replace their names and individual identities. Why did the Nazis do all this?

The main reason for the dehumanization was in order to break the Jews, to destroy their individuality and self-worth. "David" disappeared, to be replaced by a hungry, compliant number, willing to do whatever it was told to.

Those who believe in the overriding importance of a state often follow the same path of minimizing the importance of the individual. An individual's life goals are sacrificed for the state. The Nazis were like this. The Communists were like this. Individuals simply don't matter.

The Importance of the Individual

Judaism, of course, radically disagrees with this radical "statist" approach. Each and every human being is created in the image of God, possessing intrinsic holiness. Individuals cannot be sacrificed for the greater good of society. Our individual lives matter.

And our actions matter. We are not simply "dust in the wind." Our lives are not meaningless. Far from it, our souls are immortal and our good choices and positive actions affect eternity — and are never forgotten.

Many people today feel that their lives are, essentially, unimportant, and therefore they don't try to do anything particularly important with their lives.

When individuals realize their own worth, they make better choices. They rise beyond their fears and frustrations and act nobly. They care for others. They give. They contribute, because they know that their contributions are important. They act well, because they feel, deep down, that in some way their actions will be remembered.

Reminders

Modern society tends to blind us to our individual importance.

The media focuses on celebrities. Normal people are usually ignored, and their importance is subtly downplayed. Even the family no longer provides people with reminders of their intrinsic importance — people often live in different cities than their parents do, and family bonds are weaker than they were in the past.

We need to be reminded that our lives *are* important. That we *will* be remembered. That the world will take note, in some way, that we lived. That we died. That our lives had meaning. Throughout history, graves and tombstones have provided a unique and powerful lesson that our lives mattered. In describing his desire for a burial and a tombstone, one commentator put it simply:

> All I really wanted was a witness. To say I was. To say, daft as it still sounds, maybe I am.[39]

A burial plot provides this witness. The person lived, loved, tried his best — and returned to his Maker.

Compare this to cremation. Not surprisingly, a large percentage of those who choose cremation also request that their ashes be scattered.[40] Scattering ashes is appealing since it is cheaper (you don't have to pay for a burial plot or a cremation niche) and the views can be beautiful (ashes are often scattered in the sea or in nature). But what does scattering do to memory?

> There is a certain irony in the scattering of ashes, given that at one time (in the mid-1800s) only the ashes of cremated criminals were scattered in order to show the severity of their criminal punishment.
>
> Scattering ashes ... began with "impious miscreants ... In order to destroy the memory of the past ..."[41]

---

39 Lynch, *The Undertaking*, 199.
40 Some claim that over 40 percent are presently scattered. See D. A. Roth, "Cremation: A Sometimes Difficult Subject," http://www.casket-online.com/Articles/031.cfm.
41 Schmidt, *Dust to Dust*, 27.

After ashes are scattered, there is no grave to visit. No names and dates. There is no special place declaring, "This individual lived." It is as if the world is stating, "This person didn't really exist."

Parallel to the cremation fad, in certain parts of Europe, funeral practices are gradually disappearing: Dead bodies are taken directly from the hospital to the municipal crematoriums, the ashes are scattered, and there are no death notices or ceremonies.

In the United States, because people generally don't want their loved ones to be completely forgotten, many cemeteries offer what is referred to as "memorialization." Rather than being scattered, an urn — sometimes an expensive one — is purchased, and the "cremains" — a euphemism for the ashes or the cremated remains — are placed in a niche in a wall. Sometimes, the ashes are buried in a small plot (roughly a third or half the size of a normal burial plot) with a headstone.

Still, ashes in a niche often don't adequately remind us of the individuals who lived and died. There are too many of them in a small area. How can a niche declare, "This individual lived, she was important!" when there are dozens and dozens of other urns above, below, and surrounding it? In other words, in the modern quest to "save space,"[42] we actually work against our need to be remembered, one of the most fundamental functions of death rites.

Individuals *are* important. When people's remains are burned, ground up, and then stuck in an urn in a columbarium, or scattered in the ocean, the subtle societal message is "Your body left no mark on the world. You left no mark on the world. You were only *dust in the wind*."

Perhaps this is why recent media articles have begun to notice a disturbing cremation trend — remains that are forgotten or abandoned. The *Seattle Times*, for example, ran a story about the Bonney-Watson Funeral Home, which reported that hundreds of

---

[42] Based on the mistaken notion that there isn't enough space on earth for cemeteries, as we deal with in chapter 12.

families have "forgotten" to pick up the cremated remains of their deceased relatives.

> As more and more people turn to cremation, such dilemmas are playing out in funeral homes across the state and nationwide. Thousands of unclaimed remains have been stacking up in cabinets and storage rooms … "It's a problem that almost every funeral home deals with," said Christine Anthony, spokeswoman for the [Oregon] state Department of Licensing, which oversees the mortuary business.[43]

A funeral home director who attended one of my talks on the subject in 2011 told the crowd that they had over two thousand unclaimed urns — and the number keeps growing.

Simply put, people intuitively realize that ashes do not have the same importance or inherent holiness as a dead body, and therefore don't afford them much respect — unlike bodies, which are almost always taken care of properly.

When individuals are given a proper burial in a small but respectful burial plot, where only *one* individual is buried, we and the world declare: "*This person lived. He mattered. He left his mark on the world. He existed. And in some way, he still does.*"

---

43 Sonia Krishman, "Thousands of Cremated Remains Go Unclaimed," *Seattle Times*, May 23, 2008, http://www.seattletimes.nwsource.com/html/localnews/2004433569_remains23m.html.

-5-
Feelings

Some people find meaning in occasionally visiting a gravesite.
Some don't.

Some people like the idea that their loved one has a permanent resting place in the world.

Some don't.

Some grandchildren never get interested in generations past. Some grandchildren do care, or — to the great surprise of their parents — will come to care later in life. Being able to visit the place where family is buried (and seeing their names and dates carved in stone) touches them deeply.

Some people don't need to visit graves.

Some do.

Those who don't care about visiting graves are rarely bothered when burial is chosen.

Those who *do* care about visiting graves are deeply hurt when cremation is chosen.

Family Feud

Jon and Debbie's father had run away when they were little. Their mother, Beth, decided early on that she would do all it took to raise them properly and give them as much of a normal life as possible. Beth followed through. She was an amazing mother.

When she died, the kids were surprised that she had written them a letter to be opened immediately upon her passing. In it, she told them how much she loved them, how proud she was of them, and shared many personal thoughts. She also mentioned that she had always put them first and didn't want to suddenly become a burden to them in her death, so she asked them to arrange cremation and to scatter the ashes somewhere nice.

Jon, legitimately concerned about finances in difficult financial times, felt they should follow their mother's directions. The family didn't have much money. The simplest cremation and scattering would be cheaper.

Debbie was shocked at her mother's request and implored Jon not to agree to the cremation. "Mom only wanted cremation because she wanted to save us money and didn't want to burden us with a whole funeral and visiting a grave. But I want a grave to visit on Mother's Day. I don't want her cremated! It isn't a burden at all. I wish she had discussed this with me before …"

Times of grief are not ideal to discuss things calmly and rationally. There is confusion, anger, guilt, and exhaustion. The cremation issue turned into a mini-war. Debbie offered to pay the difference in costs, but Jon, armed with the letter, had their mother cremated. Debbie felt violated. They didn't speak for years.[44]

The cremation versus burial choice does create a surprising number of interpersonal problems in different families. Choosing burial is still the norm for most people in most situations. Even if some members of the family are open to cremation, rarely will burial offend or distance them.

Cremation is different. Even with today's greater acceptance of cremation, many people find cremation problematic, whether for emotional, psychological, traditional, or other reasons. One of the children of the deceased may be traumatized by the thought of burning their parent, or may need the closure of a funeral. Many want — or will want — a traditional graveside to visit. Choosing cremation can, in the short or long term, create friction and resentment.

Closure

Cremation seems appealing when you read the brochures. Cremation companies (sometimes called "societies") speak about simplicity, nature, and low-cost alternatives. Yet many families who choose cremation are surprised by the lack of closure that occurs. People describe it as if the deceased "just disappeared." There is nothing left. Nowhere to go, no place of "rest."

A *Newsweek* magazine article many years ago[45] delineated the changing place of death in human society over the millennium. Long ago, death was a familiar, expected reality. Slow changes occurred over time:

> By the mid-twentieth century, death was rapidly disappearing from public view in the industrialized Western

---

44 Based on a true story told to the author.
45 May 1, 1978, 41.

nations. [French social historian Philippe] Aries saw the increasing popularity of cremation as a confirmation of his opinion that the "once familiar face of death has become, in Western societies, something shameful and forbidden." ...

The more we reduce the impact of death and the opportunity to grieve, the more psychological complications tend to arise over a longer period than we might normally expect. One of the reasons for the popularity of cremation is the brevity of the ceremony. This tends to "short circuit" the expression of grief and can result in a complication of the later grieving process.[46]

Regrets

Few families will ever have second thoughts about giving their parent a proper burial. It is respectful, peaceful, and comforting. Many families, however, come to regret their decision to cremate their recently departed loved ones. With little time to think calmly, and little information available, they got caught up in the modern cremation fad.

Later on, they wish there was a grave to visit.

Sadly, there is no second chance to fix the mistake.

Cremation cannot be undone.

---

46 Donald Howard, *Burial or Cremation: Does It Matter?* (New York: Banner of Truth Press, 2001), 25.

-6-
Symbolism and Meaning of Burial and Cremation

Every society lives by its own set of symbols. With limited time and words at our disposal, we need common context to understand each other. We rely on these symbols daily. My computer has neither a trash can, nor an inbox, nor files, but Microsoft Outlook seems to think it does — and could not function without some system of universal associations.

Symbolism is much more important than merely saving time. Aristotle wrote, "The greatest thing, by far, is to be a master of symbolism.[47] It is the one thing that cannot be learned; and it is also a sign of genius."[48] Why? Symbols reflect how we look at life, how we frame it and give it meaning. When society chooses its

---

47 Sometimes translated as "metaphor."
48 *De Poetica*, 322 BCE, http://www.cod.edu/people/faculty/bobtam/website/metaphor.htm.

symbols, it is defining its values. Whether in a word, phrase, picture, or even in an underlying assumption, symbols help remind us what is important. Those who share symbols are bound together, for instance, by a flag or a language or a role model. Symbolism helps us make sense of the universe and of our place in it.

The Meaning of Burial

When a body is buried, the ground is opened up. A tear in the earth appears. The gaping hole declares, "Something is not right here — there is a tear in the human fabric of life. Take note, world, don't rush through this moment. Recognize the loss. Remember the life."

When the body is gently placed in the ground, a new message is given — the calm return to nature, the source of life. After decades of denying our mortality,

> Americans are starting to accept, if not embrace, this fundamental fact of biology: that the natural end of all life is decomposition and decay. Instead of fighting it at almost all cost as we have for the better part of the last century — with toxic chemicals, bulletproof metal caskets, and the concrete bunker that is the burial vault, all of which will only delay, not halt, the inevitable — we're finally seeing the wisdom of allowing Mother Nature to run her natural course.[49]

The earth, the dirt, is indeed "the Mother of All Life." The earth provides our sustenance, like a mother who gives birth to and feeds her young. And to it all creatures return, to begin the cycle once again.[50]

---

49 Mark Harris, *Grave Matters: A Journey through the Modern Funeral Industry to a Natural Way of Burial* (New York: Scribner, 2007), 186.
50 Tucazinsky, *Gesher HaChaim*, 1:119.

As British dramatist Francis Beaumont put it,

> Upon my buried body lay
> Lightly, gently, earth.[51]

The gradual process of returning to the soil reflects "the inner meaning of death. The passing of one generation allows the sprouting of another, and the living are nourished and inspired by the legacy of the dead. Our forebears are the soil from which we sprout — even in their death, they are a source of life."[52]

It is no surprise that environmentalists appreciate the beauty and symmetry of burial. Author and naturalist Aldo Leopold wrote:

> A rock decays and forms soil. In the soil grows an oak, which bears an acorn, which feeds a squirrel, which feeds an Indian, who ultimately lays him down in his last sleep to grow another oak.[53]

Environmentalist Edward Abbey goes further:

> [After] the moment of death ... we should get ... out of the way, with our bodies decently planted in the earth to nourish other forms of life — weeds, flowers, shrubs, trees, which support other forms of life, which support the ongoing human pageant — the lives of our children. That seems good enough to me.[54]

---

51 Francis Beaumont and John Fletcher, *The Maid's Tragedy*, ed. T. W. Craik (Manchester: Manchester University Press, 1999), II:i.

52 Rabbi Aaron Moss, "Cremation: What Is the Jewish View?" *Jewish Magazine*, March 2007, http://www.jewishmag.com/112mag/cremation/cremation.htm.

53 Aldo Leopold, *For the Health of the Land: Previously Unpublished Essays and Other Writings*, ed. J. Baird Callicott and Eric T. Freyfogle (Washington, DC: Island Press, 1999).

54 Bob Butz, *Going Out Green: One Man's Adventure Planning His Own Natural Burial* (Traverse City, MI: Spirituality & Health Books, 2009), 5.

Green grass. Flowers. Shade trees. Heartfelt monuments. Reminders of births and deaths. References to the love between generations. Rest and tranquility, a refuge from the frenetic pace of modern life and its struggles … There is poetry to the grave. The very word *cemetery* comes from the Greek *koimeteria,* "temporary sleeping places." The imagery is beautiful. Calm sleep. A subtle promise, somehow, in some way, of rebirth.

As English Romantic poet Percy Bysshe Shelley put it,

> The cemetery is an open space among the ruins, covered in winter with violets and daisies.
> It might make one in love with death, to think that one should be buried in so sweet a place.[55]

Burial offers meaningful symbols of a calm return to Earth, the cycle of nature, giving back what we received — and of accepting the rhythm of life, death, and the universe.

The Meaning of Cremation

In his pivotal 1970 masterpiece, "The Pursuit of Loneliness," Professor Philip Slater described what he called "the toilet assumption." Instead of dealing with societal problems, we often push them off to the side where we can't see them. We convince ourselves that once something is flushed down the toilet and out of our view, it's taken care of. Nothing more to worry about — "out of sight, out of mind."

We certainly benefit from the ease and cleanliness of modern toilets, and yet are sometimes disadvantaged by our constant desire to avoid unpleasantness. We are so used to the unpleasantness of life disappearing quickly with a simple flush that we are less able to deal with difficulties when we have no choice.

---

55   Percy Bysshe Shelley, *Adonais* (Nabu Press, 2010), 57.

Undertaker Thomas Lynch explained:

> And just as bringing the crapper indoors has made feces an embarrassment, pushing the dead and dying out has made death one ... Often I am asked to deal with the late uncle in the same way ... out of sight, out of mind. Make it go away, disappear. Push the button, pull the chain, get on with life ... And to ignore our excrement might be good form, while to ignore our mortality creates an "imbalance," a kind of spiritual irregularity, psychic impaction, a bunging up of our humanity, a denial of our very nature.[56]

Cremation reflects and promotes a worldview of death-denial. People don't like funerals, funeral homes, or cemetery visits. So modernity has found a way of making the process faster and less disturbing: pull on the flusher, figuratively speaking. Part of the appeal of cremation is its efficiency. Simple. Quick. To the point.

The problem is that the bodies of our parents and grandparents are the same bodies that gave birth to us, held us, worked hard to provide for us, and cried for us. They are not meant to be flushed or cremated away.

Some human experiences should not be so quick and efficient.

In fact, the problematic message of cremation extends even further. Eastern religions and ancient pagan Greeks viewed fire as a type of purifier. Monotheistic teachings see things quite differently. In monotheistic thought, it is water that purifies (think of a *mikveh* — a ritual bath). Fire punishes. Instead of cleansing an object — literally or figuratively — fire destroys it, leaving nothing left. In fact, putting something to the flames is considered such a terrible punishment that the Bible reserves it for the worst type of crimes.

---

56 Lynch, *The Undertaking*, 37.

Here are a few examples[57]:

- When the ancient Hebrews built the golden calf, they incurred God's wrath. Moses did the harshest thing he could to eliminate the idol: he burned it.[58]
- When the evil Korach and his supporters rebelled, God sent fire to punish them.[59]
- God commanded that pagan idols be destroyed with fire.[60]

The Bible is consistent in the imagery and symbolism of burning. When Sodom and Gomorrah would not change their evil ways,

> God rained upon Sodom and upon Gomorrah brimstone and fire ... out of heaven.[61]

---

57 Other examples abound. For instance, Leviticus 20:14 and 21:9, Joshua 7:15–25, 2 Kings 10:26, Jeremiah 29:22, and Judges 15:6. Not having a proper burial was considered a great dishonor; see 1 Kings 21:23–24 and Psalms 83:9–10.

It is important to note the case of King Saul in 1 Samuel 31:11–13. Saul is wounded and commits suicide (usually forbidden by Jewish law, here an exceptional case in order to prevent the Philistines from capturing and disgracing the king of Israel). The Philistines, showing tremendous disregard for the honor of a king, impale his body (as well as those of his sons) and gruesomely display it publicly. The Jews of Jabesh Gilead secretly retrieve the bodies, "burn them," and bury the bones.

This episode has occasionally been used as a justification for cremation, but mistakenly so. First of all, grammatically it is not clear what was burned. Traditionally, kings' possessions were burned to prevent others from using them, and perhaps it was Saul's clothes that were burned in this verse, not his body — as was done in other cases. Or perhaps because the bodies had already decomposed and become infested, the Jews burned the remaining putrid flesh and buried the bones. This was not cremation — but was rather a last resort, a desperate attempt to avoid further desecration, dealing with a dangerous emergency situation and the honor of a king. They quickly buried whatever could be buried, thus actually showing the importance the people of the time attached to burial.

58 Exodus 32:20.
59 Numbers 16:35.
60 Deuteronomy 7:25.
61 Genesis 19:24.

When Nadab and Abihu brought a strange fire into the Tabernacle,

> and there went out fire from the Lord, and devoured them, and they died.[62]

When the evil Korach and his followers rebelled against Moses,

> and there came out a fire from God, and consumed the two hundred and fifty men.[63]

In dealing with idol worship, the Bible screams:

> You shall burn the graven images of their gods …[64]

> And they brought forth the images out of the house of Baal, and burned them.[65]

Burial represents a positive metaphor of acceptance and a calm return to the earth.

From time immemorial, in the West, fire has symbolized destruction, judgment, and Divine anger. The underlying message of cremation is one of efficiency, violence, and judgment:

- Efficiency: Why be patient when I can do things faster?
- Violence: Why be passive when I can actively burn and destroy?
- Judgment: Why allow nature to slowly take its course when I can exert control?

Do we burn things we love? Think back to your first pet:

---

62 Leviticus 10:1–2.
63 Numbers 16:35.
64 Deuteronomy 7:25.
65 2 Kings 10:26.

We burned the trash and buried the treasure. That is why, faced with life's first lessons in mortality — the dead kitten or bunny rabbit, or dead bird fallen from its nest on high — good parents search out shoe boxes and shovels instead of kindling wood or barbecues ...[66]

Two Attitudes

Burial and cremation usually reflect two radically different attitudes, and two mutually exclusive ways of seeing the world and understanding our place in it.

Decomposition and burning are vastly different from one another and, in many ways, complete opposites. Decomposition of a plant or living creature creates fertilizer. The intrinsic elements of the matter are not changed — rather they are given back to the ground. No wonder that the Talmud compares burial to a type of planting.[67]

Cremation, on the other hand, leaves only burnt ashes, its elements forever changed and almost entirely burnt off.[68] Try burning a seed before planting it — nothing will grow. In choosing cremation, humanity shows its power, but to what end?

The message of cremation is to side with man as conqueror, using fire and technology to interfere with and control nature — rather than peacefully accept it.

The message of burial is one of respect for the cycle of nature. When burying the remains of our loved ones, we calmly return what we have received. Burial reflects the rhythm of the universe.

---

66 Lynch, *The Undertaking*, 96.
67 Tractate *Sanhedrin* 90b and *Ketubot* 111b.
68 Tucazinsky, *Gesher HaChaim*, 1:117.

-7-

Graves Are for the Living

In the West today, the elderly are often regarded as an annoyance or as the punch line of an unkind joke. They are no longer "contributing" members of society. Their need for assistance drains our time. Their need for medical care drains our money.

Still, we will care for them. It is the right thing to do. And we hope and trust that the same will be done for us when the time comes.

But what about the dead? The dead offer us, literally, nothing. Burials take time, cost money, and use land. No wonder many today consider the dead to be a nuisance. Investing in them seems like a waste.

Bowling Alone

One of the most insightful books on the modern condition that I've read is *Bowling Alone* by Harvard University's eminent political scientist, Robert Putnam.[69] He demonstrates that contemporary culture has largely lost its sense of community. Membership in local organizations is down. Church and synagogue attendance is down. Participation in communal activities is down. More and more people are even bowling alone, to cite one noteworthy example.

There are many reasons for the decline of the community. One common explanation is the allure of individual freedom. *I want to do whatever I want, however I want, whenever I want.* Being part of a community, on the other hand, obligates certain standards of behavior. When I am part of a community, my freedoms are more limited. Some run away from community obligations and prefer "bowling alone."

But in the end, everyone loses. When one person withdraws, others lose his or her potential contribution to society. The absent individual loses even more. The lonely bowler misses out on the richness of life. On developing close friendships and bonds formed through shared interests and activities. On the depth of being part of community. Of giving and receiving. Of adding a "we" to the "me."

Jefferson versus Madison

Being part of a community is important, most would agree. But what does community have to do with the dead?

According to Thomas Jefferson, very little: "The earth belongs to the living and not to the dead," he wrote to James Madison in

---

[69] New York: Simon & Schuster, 1995.

1789.[70] Were they discussing the appropriateness of providing land for cemeteries? No.

The question they were actually discussing was: Does government have the right to borrow money, thus indebting future generations? Jefferson argued that a generation as yet unborn cannot be forced to repay money it never agreed to borrow in the first place. How can the past obligate the future? On this point, Thomas Paine agreed when he said, "I am contending for the rights of the living, and against their being ... controlled ... [by the] authority of the dead."[71]

Madison understood things differently. Countries and peoples cannot simply be reinvented every generation. Society is comparable to a movie, not a snapshot, to use a modern analogy. One generation builds buildings, invests in agriculture, develops technologies, and creates literature and art ... and future generations benefit greatly from all of these: "The improvements made by the dead form a debt against the living, who take the benefit of them," he declared.

Because the next generation by definition benefits (usually greatly) from the past, the two are closely connected to each other, and the present generation retains certain obligations to the past. Edmund Burke perhaps expressed this idea best when he said that society is "a partnership not only between those who are living, but between those who are living, those who are dead, and those who are yet to be born."[72]

This idea, if understood correctly, is profound:

The living have a stake in the future, and the deceased have a stake in the present.

---

70 *The Writings of Thomas Jefferson*, ed. H.A. Washington (New York, 1861), 359.
71 Thomas Paine, *The Rights of Man*, Independence Hall Association in Philadelphia: USHistory.org, http://www.ushistory.org/paine/rights/c1-010.htm.
72 These paragraphs are inspired by Joseph Bottum's "Death & Politics," *First Things*, July 2007, http://www.firstthings.com/article/2009/02/001-death--politics-29.

A new generation should not see itself as detached from the past. Society is not reborn every generation, creating its identity and political and social systems from scratch. Rather, we are intimately connected to the past and the future. Those not yet born have an interest in how we lead our lives and what we do, for our decisions deeply affect them. And those already gone, too, have a stake in the present: They built the world we inherited and handed it over as a trust. Our entire lives are built on the foundation of theirs.

Madison and Burke point to something that Jews often intrinsically understand. Most Jews feel a deep connection to the Jewish past (for instance, remembrance of the Holocaust) and the future (for example, the safety and success of the State of Israel). When we think of being Jewish, we don't think only of those alive today. We are one chapter in an ongoing epic drama of history. We invest our time and money in preservation of the past and protecting the future … because we (correctly) feel obligated to do so. We are part of something bigger than ourselves, and bigger than any one generation.

Eat, Drink, and Be Merry

Compare this idea — that our lives are part of an ongoing community including the living, the dead, and the as-yet unborn — to a phrase you may have heard of: "Eat, drink, and be merry for tomorrow we die." The idea, taken to its extreme, represents complete preoccupation with the present. Don't focus on the past. Don't worry about the future. Just enjoy.

Many young people get caught up in this live-for-the-day attitude. As we mature, though, we see that the depth of life includes the hopes and plans for the future. After all, my concern for the environment only makes sense if I care what future generations will do with it as well. Why bother protecting the planet now if others will simply destroy it only a few years down the road?

We also come to realize that quality of life depends on the lessons and memories of the past. I want my children to know who their grandparents were, where they came from, and what their heritage is. Connecting to the past helps us understand what is happening in the present and what our goals should be for the future.

The Milford Bridge

Connecting to the past — and to those who have passed on — is crucial to who we are and who we become.

When the bridge connecting the town of Milford, Michigan, to its cemetery collapsed, some younger folks were reluctant to pay for its repair. After all, there was another roundabout way to get to the cemetery. A much longer route, to be sure, but how often does one go to the cemetery, anyway?

Older members of the community successfully argued that the cemetery should not be cut off from the community. Their feelings were perhaps best expressed by the town's poet-undertaker, Thomas Lynch, cited above:

> A graveyard is an old agreement made
> Between the living and the living who have died
> That says we keep their names and dates alive.
> This bridge connects our daily lives to them
> And makes them, once our neighbors, neighbors once again.[73]

A beautiful thought: The deceased can remain part of our lives, and part of our community, if we will let them.

---

73 Lynch, *The Undertaking*, 121.

Imagine a society cut off from its past, where the living felt no responsibility to remember or carry on the legacy of preceding generations. What would happen?

When people build a society that is disconnected from the past, they know that the society they build will also be disconnected from the future. If I ignore those that preceded me, those that come next will ignore me as well — the cycle repeats itself. If I forget about my grandparents, will my grandchildren forget about me?

Furthermore, if those gone are forgotten, will I really care about those alive ... since they, too, will soon enough be forgotten? If I don't care about my dead parents, do I still care about my living aunts and uncles? My cousins? My siblings? If they will eventually forget me, do they really care about me now? As undertaker Lynch put it:

> The meaning of life is connected, inextricably, to the meaning of death ... mourning is a romance in reverse, and if you love, you grieve and there are no exceptions — only those that do it well and those who don't. And if death is regarded as an embarrassment or an inconvenience, if the dead are regarded as a nuisance from whom we seek hurried riddance, then life and living are in for like treatment. McFunerals, McFamilies, McMarriage, McValues.[74]

The bridges that we build to the past also connect us to each other in the present. The bridges that I maintain to the dead also connect me to myself — to the deeper, more giving, and more connected part of who I am and who I want to be.

For society to function well, people need to feel and know that they are part of something bigger than themselves, and that their lives and contributions matter. The living need to know and be

---

74 Ibid., 25.

reminded of the lives and contributions of those who have passed on. Without those reminders, we are adrift, cut off from the community of history, secretly knowing and fearing that we too will be forgotten. On the other hand, with the knowledge and reminders of generations past, we bind ourselves to the future. We acknowledge our place in history, and value our achievements as everlasting contributions to the general good.

In other words, *healthy societies require the presence of the dead.*

Community cannot be created and recreated at a moment's notice. Community needs to be protected, cherished, and cultivated. And community needs anchors. Shared history provides the most central of those anchors. Throughout history, in all cultures and societies, death rituals bring people together to speak of the past and hope for the future.

The dead help build our communities. They contribute to social cohesiveness. They remind us of our shared past and help build our shared future. By burying our dead together in communal cemeteries — rather than scattering one person's ashes alone in nature — we declare to others and remind ourselves of the importance of community — that we do not go through the journey of life alone, but together.

The dead also help build our families. When we care for our dead, bury them, and maintain and even occasionally visit their graves, we strengthen our shared bonds to the past, and thus our bonds to each other. When a grandfather or grandmother is fondly remembered, the grandchildren feel more of a connection to each other. On the other hand, when we neglect family graves, our connection to the past is weakened and our connection to family is thus weakened.

It is, in a sense, a self-fulfilling prophecy: The less important the past is to us, the less we need markers to remember it. And the less we remember it, the less important it will be to us. The opposite is, thankfully, also true. The more we remember our parents, grandparents, and previous generations, and the more reminders we have to keep them in our minds and hearts, the more we strengthen our bonds to them — and to each other.

Graves Teach

Cemeteries are not (only) for the dead. The dead are not a nuisance or a drain. Graves are not wasted land. We, the living, need them. We need them to teach us, connect us, remind us, motivate us, and obligate us.

Graves teach. They teach about life's finality. They teach us not to be overfocused on acquisitions or ego, which will disappear soon enough.

Graves connect. Through commemorating a common parent, grandparent, or ancestor, graves connect us to each other.

Graves remind. They remind us of love, devotion, and bonds that we don't always feel in the present. They remind us of the importance of the affection given from parent to child, from grandparent to grandchild.

Graves motivate. They propel us to consider what will be written on our epitaphs. They motivate us to improve as we consider, *What will be my contribution? How will I be remembered?* Perhaps Abraham Lincoln put it best when he taught that from the "honored dead" at Gettysburg, the living "take increased devotion to that cause for which they gave the last full measure of devotion."[75]

Graves obligate. They obligate us to remember. They obligate us to assure their maintenance and, occasionally perhaps visit. These obligations are healthy. We need these obligations to be fully human.

---

[75] LibertyOnline, Gettysburg Address, given November 19, 1863, on the battlefield near Gettysburg, Pennsylvania, http://libertyonline.hypermall.com/Lincoln/gettysburg.html.

The Blessing of a Burden

This last point deserves extra attention. Many parents and grandparents choose cremation because they don't want to "be a burden" to their families. While a sweet sentiment, this idea mistakenly assumes that giving proper care to the elderly and burial to the dead is an "unfair" obligation on the younger generation, who will (a) need to pay the funeral bills, or receive less inheritance; and (b) feel obligated to, on Mother's Day, a *yahrtzeit* (anniversary of the day of death), or when passing through town, come to visit the grave.

These generous elderly souls, willing to sacrifice yet again and give to their children, are actually taking something away from them. As one commentator put it,

> But if we are not to be a burden to our children, then to whom? The government? The church? The taxpayers? Whom? Were they not a burden to us — our children? And didn't the management of that burden make us feel alive and loved and helpful and capable?[76]

The next generation is not "burdened" by arranging the burial and making the occasional visit to the gravesite. They are enriched by it. They receive a final lesson in the honor and gratitude due to parents. They are reminded of their connection to their past, thus strengthening their own identity and family bonds. They are motivated to leave their own legacy. They learn the importance of community, past, present, and future.

We, the living, need the visible presence of the past — of the dead — to understand life, feel compassion, and develop continuity.

We need graves. Graves are for the living.

---

76 Lynch, *The Undertaking*, 186.

Summary of Part 1

- Research has shown that, historically, monotheists bury the dead, while polytheists and atheists choose cremation.
- The Bible and Jewish tradition are clearly and consistently pro-burial and anti-cremation, considering the burning of a body a terrible violation of the person's memory and God's image.
- Jews and the Jewish State make enormous sacrifices to provide proper Jewish burials to all.
- When Torah scrolls are damaged beyond repair, they are lovingly buried. Our bodies, partners to our souls throughout our lives, are holier than scrolls, and deserve burial as well.
- Burial emphasizes, and cremation downplays, the importance of the individual.
- Burial symbolizes the acceptance of the cycle of life, a peaceful return to nature, returning what we have received. Cremation represents one last assertion of violent control, denying death's natural process, and wishing to do away with the unpleasant ordeal as quickly as possible. Bury the pet versus burn the garbage.
- Burial rarely creates family discord. Cremation often does — and cannot be undone.
- Healthy societies need cemeteries to remind us of our mortality, connect us to our families, and teach us of the community of history.

Part 2
Practicalities

Introduction to Part 2

While we all have our philosophical moments, most of us are rational and practical people. We make our decisions based on what makes the most sense and what is most likely to work out best.

Cremation is no exception to this rule. Most people who choose cremation do so at least in part for practical reasons: it seems quick and clean, avoids leaving a gravesite unvisited due to children living far away, and seems to cost less.

In the previous section, we addressed the ideas behind burial and cremation. In this section, we will address practical concerns. As we will see, most of the assumptions and information people have about the practical aspects of cremation are questionable — and many are simply untrue.

-8-

The Process of Cremation

Many people are bothered by the idea of being buried in the ground. Decomposition seems disgusting. People don't like the idea of being "eaten by worms."

No wonder cremation seems like a better alternative, especially considering the advertising:

> Dolphins swimming in pairs. Hot air balloons. Rocky Mountain vistas. Flower-filled valleys. A beautiful young woman walking on the beach hand in hand with her smiling elderly mother as the sun sets over the horizon …

The imagery used by the modern cremation industry is impressive. It associates cremation with nature, beauty, love, and cleanliness. This type of imagery[77] has taken away much of the stigma of cremation.

---

77 One woman described how she was convinced to choose cremation: "The [attendant] explained how the casket was placed in the retort [oven], the door electrically sealed

Even the modern burning process itself seems quite benign. Consider the following typical description:

> A body is placed (usually within a coffin or other container) in the retort, which is heated to a high temperature, typically between 1,800 and 2,000 degrees Fahrenheit. The casket and body are almost completely consumed. The cremated remains (sometimes referred to as "ashes"), consisting of bone fragments and particles, usually weigh between five and eight pounds. They are processed into granule form. Start to finish, the process takes two to three hours.[78]

Upon further examination, though, it turns out that cremation is neither quick nor clean. Cremations do not happen immediately — the body usually sits around for a number of days in line, sometimes waiting for official permission to proceed. Crematory workers poke around the body to check for implants, pacemakers, and more — and physically remove them in order to protect their equipment. Only then can the cremation begin.

Furthermore, reading positive stories and descriptions like those above, one could almost forget that *cremate* is simply a fancy

---

for four hours. 'Afterward the ashes are gathered and sealed in a container to be placed in a niche in the chapel or given to the relatives.' I was still not satisfied. 'Does it burn?' I asked. 'Like a bonfire?' The thought of flames touching someone I loved, charring his beauty, was insupportable. The old man asked, 'Have you ever looked into the sun? You know how bright and clear it is. That is what surrounds the body and consumes it. Light, like the sun.'

"Light, like the sun. A sense of triumph came over me. Sunlight over Father working in his garden. Sunlight on his white head as he sat on the terrace reading. The warmth of sunlight bringing life to growing things, falling benignly on the aging. 'When his time comes, I shall bring him here'" (Frances Newton, "Light, Like the Sun," Funeral Consumers Alliance, November 26, 2007, http://www.funerals.org/faq/73-light-like-the-sun).

78 Composite of several industry descriptions. An Internet search will reveal many similar descriptions.

word for *burn*.[79] The word *burn* has too many negative associations when used in the context of human death, so the industry prefers not to use it. Cremationists have even ceased using the word *incinerator* because the same type of machine is used for burning trash. It is interesting to note which words are used by the industry today, disconnecting what actually happens from what they want us to think about:

Euphemism	Original Word
Cremains / cremated remains	Ashes
Garden of Remembrance	Crematorium grounds
Process	Grind / pulverize
Retort / chamber	Oven / cremator / incinerator

In a similar vein, modern cremationists seek to distance themselves as much as possible from ancient (and modern) open-air cremations. One Christian critique of cremation shows why:

> I am convinced that if Christians in America and Europe could stand with me beside the "holy" River Bagmati in Kathmandu, Nepal, and observe the burning of the body of a Hindu following the performance of the Hindu death rituals, they would cast aside in repulsion every thought of cremation being … acceptable … Just five days ago I stood three or so feet from a burning corpse with a missionary pastor from Singapore and his wife who were visiting us. The head was already burnt beyond recognition and the skull split open due to internal expansion from the heat of the fire. The lower legs and feet were unscorched, as they were protruding from the pile of burning wood

---

79 In fact, the word *cremation* actually comes from the Latin word *cremo*, which means "to burn."

and stubble upon which the man's body lay. The professional Hindu burners were poking the body from time to time to keep the members in the fire and adding stubble and wood as needed. The bones were contracting and popping; the bodily organs were frying and the juices sizzling in the intense heat. My wife, a nurse with experience in a leprosy hospital and also in an intensive care ward, stood with another friend observing the ghastly sight from a distance, unwilling to come closer. The air for a hundred yards or more was filled with the unmistakable stench of burning flesh.[80] When the fire had burnt most of the body, the ashes and remaining members were shoved into the river. This is cremation as has been practiced ... for untold centuries ..."[81]

By using a closed oven instead of an open fire, disturbing sounds, smells, and images suddenly seem to not exist. Interestingly, in modern cremation literature, almost nothing is said about what actually happens to the body of the deceased. Those who choose cremation usually prefer not to think about it.

Modern ovens only mask the process and its corresponding sounds and smells. In the chamber, nothing has changed.

---

80 "... What does burning human flesh smell like? ... You'll know it when you smell it ... Burning skin has a charcoal-like smell, while setting hair on fire produces a sulfurous odor ... The smell of burnt hair can cling to the nostrils for days ... Unless someone's standing at the door of the actual cremator, however, it's unlikely anyone will catch a whiff. Modern cremation systems feature smoke stacks and exhaust fans that remove almost all odor ... It's easier to recognize the smell than to describe it. Emergency workers and survivors of war atrocities say charred flesh simply smells like nothing else ... J.D. Salinger, who helped liberate concentration camps in World War II, told his daughter, 'You never really get the smell of burning flesh out of your nose entirely. No matter how long you live'" (Michelle Tsai, "Bar-B-You: What's the Smell of Burning Human Flesh?" *Slate Magazine*, March 26, 2007, http://www.slate.com/id/2162676/).

81 David Cloud, "Cremation — What Does God Think?" *Baptist Challenge*, March 1989.

The body itself does not calmly fade into oblivion as it is being burned. It moves about,[82] with expansion and contraction of muscles and sinews common due to the intense heat. As described by W. E. D. Evans in *The Chemistry of Death*:

> The coffin is introduced into the furnace where it rapidly catches fire, bulges and wraps, and the coffin sides may collapse and fall, exposing the remains to the direct effect of the flames. The skin and hair at once scorch, char and burn ... the muscles slowly contract, and there may be a steady divarication of the thighs with gradually developing flexion of the limbs ... Occasionally there is swelling of the abdomen before the skin and abdominal muscles char and split; the swelling is due to the formation of steam and the expansion of gases in the abdominal contents. Destruction of the soft tissues gradually exposes parts of the skeleton. The skull is soon devoid of covering, then the bones of limbs appear, commencing at the extremities of the limbs where they are relatively poorly covered by muscles or fat, and the ribs also become exposed. The small bones of the digits, wrists and ankles remain united by their ligaments for a surprising length of time, maintaining their anatomical relationship even though the hands and feet fall away from the adjacent long bones. The abdominal contents burn fairly slowly, and the lungs more slowly still ... the brain is especially resistant to

---

82 "Think of the horrors ... of the crisping, crackling, roasting, steaming, shriveling, blazing features and hands that yesterday were your soul's delight. Think of exploding cadavers. Think of the stench of burning flesh and hair. Think of the smoke. Think of the bubbling brains. Then you will be gripped by 'paralyzing horror' at even the thought of 'submitting the remains of ... dear departed relatives to its sizzling process.' Cremation [is], in a word, repulsive: 'There is nothing beautiful in being shoved in to an oven, and scientifically barbecued by a patented furnace'" (Prothero, *Purified by Fire*, 67).

> complete combustion during cremation of the body. Even when the vault of the skull has broken and fallen away, the brain has been seen as a dark, fused mass with rather sticky consistency, and the organ may persist in this form for most of the time required for the destruction of the remains ... Eventually the spine becomes visible as the viscera disappear; the bones glow whitely [sic] in the flames, and the skeleton falls apart. Some bones fragment into pieces of various sizes while other bones remain whole.[83]

Put simply, cremation is not peaceful, quiet, or calm. It is a harsh, smelly, loud act of violence committed against the body of a recently deceased loved one.

The Separation

Once the burning is complete and the remains cool down, the next step is to separate nonbone fragments from the rest of the remains.

> All organic bone fragments, which are very brittle, as well as non-consumed metal items are "swept" into the back of the cremation chamber and into a stainless steel cooling pan. All non-consumed items, like metal from clothing, hip joints, and bridge work, are separated from the cremated remains. This separation is accomplished through visual inspection as well as using a strong magnet for smaller and minute metallic objects

---

83 W. E. D. Evans, *The Chemistry of Death* (Springfield, IL: Charles C. Thomas Publishers, 1963), 83–85, quoted in Schmidt, *Dust to Dust*, 23.

... Remaining bone fragments are then processed in a machine to a consistent size ...[84]

In other words, a lowly paid crematory worker sifts through the remains by hand and with the aid of a magnet in order to separate out any nonbone material.

Processing

Next, the bone fragments are swept out and the crematory operator "processes them" into fine granules. Alternatively known as pulverizing or grinding, these processors use a rotating or grinding mechanism to chop the bones down to very fine powder. This is, of course, a refinement of simpler techniques: they used to pulverize remains with a hammer or board, or use handheld grinders.

Perhaps repulsed by the idea of grinding Grandma, the ancient Greeks and Romans did not pulverize bones,[85] thus explaining why their urns were larger than modern ones. Today, grinding is standard practice in the United States and Western Europe.

Mixed Remains

With the same oven being used for body after body, it is not surprising that residue from others' remains, as well as soot from the flame, wood from the casket,[86] particles from the firebrick, and other materials *do* get mixed up with the remains of the deceased:

---

84 Cremation Society of Southern Wisconsin, "Questions about the Cremation Process," http://www.csofswi.com/_mgxroot/page_10730.php.
85 Even today, the Japanese and Taiwanese generally don't grind bones.
86 Consider also: "Bodies are sometimes cremated inside a container, such as a wooden casket used for a viewing. In that case, wood ash and the casket's latches and handles might get mingled with the remains ..." (Melonyce McAfee, "I'm Burning Up — How Much Will My Ashes Weigh?" *Slate Magazine*, July 26, 2006, http://www.slate.com/id/2146542/).

Although the attendants attempt to remove all of the remains, a small portion will be left inside the cremation chamber, and subsequently mingled with the next body to be cremated.[87]

The problem is serious enough that California law requires written acknowledgment of the following disclosure when cremation is to take place:

> The human body burns with the casket, container, or other material in the cremation chamber. Some bone fragments are not combustible at the incineration temperature and, as a result, remain in the cremation chamber. During the cremation, the contents of the chamber may be moved to facilitate incineration. The chamber is composed of ceramic or other material which disintegrates slightly during each cremation, and the product of that disintegration is co-mingled with the cremated remains. Nearly all of the contents of the cremation chamber, consisting of the cremated remains, disintegrated chamber material, and small amounts of residue from previous cremations, are removed together and crushed, pulverized, or ground to facilitate inurnment or scattering. Some residue remains in the cracks and uneven places of the chamber ...[88]

---

87   Religioustolerance.org, http://www.religioustolerance.org/crematio.htm. Similarly, the *New World Encyclopedia* reports: "An unavoidable consequence of cremation is that a tiny residue of bodily remains is left in the chamber after cremation and mixes with subsequent cremations" (*New World Encyclopedia*, s.v. "Cremation," http://www.newworldencyclopedia.org/entry/Cremation).

88   State of California Department of Consumer Affairs: Cemetery and Funeral Bureau, "Consumer Guide to Funeral & Cemetery Purchases," http://www.cfb.ca.gov/consumer/funeral.shtml.

The Ground or the Oven?

Some people are squeamish about burial. Certainly, decomposition is not pretty to contemplate. Nevertheless, in light of the above, cremation hardly seems any better.[89]

Furthermore, decomposition is a natural process that occurs to all (formerly) living beings. Though not pretty, it is the natural way of the earth. On the other hand, cremation is loud, violent, disgusting, and artificial.

---

89 Occasionally, things are even worse than described above: "Obese bodies still emit heavy black smoke and flames when cremated" (Kenneth V. Iserson, *Death to Dust: What Happens to Dead Bodies?* [Tucson, AZ: Galen Press, 1999], 262), and "Sometimes things go wrong ... Silicone breast implants can cause problems during a cremation. Remains of the body can stick to it, meaning the body may be lumpy instead of turning to a fine ash" (Sarah Matthews, "Cremation: Burn, Baby, Burn," Free Online Library, August 7, 2007, http://www.thefreelibrary.com/Cremation+Burn,+Baby,+Burn-a01073972282).

-9-
Mobility

Life used to be simpler. Most people kept the same jobs for their whole lives. They had the same friends for their whole lives. And they used to live in the same town as their parents, grandparents, and great-grandparents.

At the cemetery, each family had its own plot. There is something beautiful about the way things were. When the kids lived in the same town as the deceased parents, one could easily visit the cemetery and pay respects on a birthday, Mother's Day, or a *yahrtzeit* (anniversary of the day of death), finding solace and reminding oneself of love and memories shared.

Things have changed.

It is a mobile world. People change jobs, careers — and cities — more than any time in history. Fewer and fewer people live in the same towns that they grew up in. In dealing with death, we moderns ask ourselves:

> Where are my parents going to be buried? In New York, where they spent their lives? In Florida, where they

retired to? In California, where I live, so that they'll be close by? What about the cities my siblings live in? And what happens when I move, or retire?

Since people today move around so much, isn't it better to cremate and thus have the remains mobile, so that they can "come along" wherever we go? Or scatter the remains in nature?

In the short term, choosing cremation due to mobility issues seems to make a lot of sense — modern mobility certainly makes cemetery visitation much harder.

However, in order to best grapple with this question, we need to think about the long-term.

How Long Will the Remains Remain in the Family?

Many people don't regard cremated remains with much reverence, and cremated remains are simply not treated as seriously as a body. One indication of this is the fact that with the recent surge in cremations, there has also been a surge in the number of unclaimed urns.

One undertaker writes of having large numbers of urns to deal with. When they sent out letters threatening monthly fees for warehousing, relatives suddenly appeared:

> Some grinned broadly and talked of the weather, taking up the ashes as one would something from a hardware store or baggage claim, tossing it into the trunk of their car like corn flakes or bird seed ... "What do I want with her ashes?" one woman asked, clearly mindless of the possibility that, however little her dead mother's ashes meant to her, they might mean even less to me.[90]

---

90   Lynch, *The Undertaking*, 91.

The problem is so significant that funeral industry entrepreneur Jason B. Rew recently created a new company, National Cremation Storage (NCS), to help find a solution. When he announced the opening of the country's only centralized secure storage and scattering services for the nation's unclaimed cremated human remains, he explained, "While the concept of unclaimed remains may be hard to fathom, it happens every day ... Funeral home and crematory owners are left with the task of attempting to place these unclaimed remains with their intended recipients, and maintaining these remains for indefinite periods of time ..."[91]

Another commentator noted that "as the number of cremations in the United States rises, so does the number of abandoned urns, either lying unclaimed in funeral homes or found in attics and basements after relatives of the deceased have passed on themselves."[92]

Let us say that a couple has three children. They decide on cremation. Either the children divide the ashes up into mini-urns, or they take turns: First year, the brother. Next year the sister. In more than a few cases, no one really *wants* the remains in their home — it seems creepy, actually — but they feel guilty and acquiesce.

What will they do with the urn, exactly?

Perhaps it will go on the mantle. Perhaps over the fireplace or on the shelf near the television. It is common for urns to be the butt of jokes and disrespect. Since not everyone is comfortable with remains of the dead in their living room, the urn often eventually gets "exiled" to a storage closet, the basement, or a corner — out of sight and mind.

Even when the children *do* find an appropriate place for the remains of their deceased parents, how long will they keep them for? Until they switch jobs and move? Until they retire? What will they

---

91 Funeral Services Provider, "Cremation Storage Service for Unclaimed Cremated Remains," http://funeralservicesprovider.com/blog/index.php/2009/06/20/cremation-storage-service-for-unclaimed-cremated-remains/.

92 Matthews, "Cremation: Burn, Baby, Burn," August 7, 2007.

do with them then? And when, in ten or twenty years, they are no longer living independently, will their children want the remains? Will they take them? What will *they* do with the remains?

Within a relatively short period of time, the number of urns can add up. Along with the antique china, family pictures, and other heirlooms passed from generation to generation, how many urns will be passed on? For how long?

The point is that our homes and families are simply not designed for long term storage of cremated remains. At some point, they are likely to be placed in an inappropriate place, forgotten, or ignored. In *all* cases, the home option is only temporary anyway. In a few years, the children or grandchildren will inevitably get rid of the urn that they don't want or can no longer keep. At that point, often the remains will not be treated with respect.

Modern mobility does indeed present a challenge. Cemeteries are farther away and harder to visit. But cremation is not the answer. Cremation tends to *decrease* reverence for the deceased's remains. And cremated remains are eventually, in this generation or the next, thrown out, scattered, or buried somewhere anyway, usually with no marker or possibility of remembrance or visitation at all.

Few Visitors or No Visitors?

The silver lining of mobility is that we travel more often, more easily, and more cheaply than ever, so families that *do* want to plan visitations can do so easily. This is an important note, because even if a child doesn't care about visiting graves, perhaps his or her children or grandchildren will. At some point later in life, it may be emotionally significant for them. This has happened in countless families. Why not leave the possibility open to the future?

Visiting a gravesite is an important and moving thing to do. It shows respect for the deceased and connects us to our past, thus reinforcing our family bonds.

But even in the cases where gravesite visitation will rarely or *never* occur, the body is not pushed away in the storage room or thrown away. As we saw in the case of Moses,[93] burial is the right choice even when it doesn't seem like there will be any visitors — the body is at rest, and has found a permanent home.

---

93 As mentioned in chapter 1, God buried Moses and hid the location of his grave — indicating that burial is the right thing to do even when there will be no visitors.

-10-
Scandals and More

In the 1980s one scattering company repeatedly dumped ashes in a landfill — after all, it's cheaper than actually scattering them. In June 26, 2001, bodies that should have been cremated long before were found in a New Haven funeral home. On June 20, 2003, in Toledo, Ohio, eight bodies slated for cremation were found in the basement of a funeral home months after the supposed date of cremation. On February 12, 2002, California resident Michael Brown was arrested on 154 counts of embezzlement and mutilation of human corpses. Instead of cremating the remains, as he agreed to, he sold them for body parts. Five days later, on Sunday, February 17, 2002, the *New York Times* ran its first story about the Tri-State Crematory scandal in Noble, Georgia. Three hundred and fourteen bodies, meant to have been cremated, were left out in sheds, stacked on top of each other, and never cremated.

These are only a few of the scandals that have ripped the cremation industry in recent years. While there have certainly been problems in cemeteries, scandals in the cremation industry seem much more common.⁹⁴ Why are there so many cremation scandals?

While there are many reasons contributing to the phenomenon, two main explanations seem to bear the greatest responsibility: (1) There is very little regulation of the cremation industry; and (2) it is impossible to identify ashes once a body is cremated, so relatives can easily be fooled into accepting the wrong ones.

As one writer put it:

> The dead don't have the law on their side. Regulation of the death industry is shoddy and spotty, with crematories low on the list of priorities.⁹⁵

The AARP (American Association of Retired Persons) ran a major article on crematory scandals in their July 3, 2006 *AARP Bulletin*. Sharon Hermanson, senior policy adviser for AARP's Public Policy Institute, noted that

> more comprehensive cremation laws are needed to address issues such as licensing, inspections, record-keeping, disposition and identification of remains and penalties for violations. As a result it's getting more difficult for consumers to know what to expect.⁹⁶

Cremation industry spokespeople insist that cases of fraud and switches of remains are rare, but the media has revealed numerous ones — and of course it stands to reason that the vast majority of problems are never discovered.⁹⁷

---

94 Kenneth Iserson's *Death to Dust* lists many other cases on pages 264–265.
95 Fred Rosen, *Cremation in America* (Amherst, NY: Prometheus Books, 2004), 21.
96 Sharon Hermanson, *AARP Bulletin*, July 3, 2006.
97 The difficulty in identifying cremated remains can sometimes hamper or prevent criminal investigations: "There is no telling how many cases ... exist in the annals of the U.S. criminal justice system in which a murderer had a body cremated to cover up the crime. In the nineteenth century ... when murderers wanted to get rid of the body, they usually did it by burial or drowning ... In the twentieth and twenty-first centuries, however, with cremation more common, it would make perfect sense for

The AARP identifies the case of Kimberly Carroll of Phoenix, Arizona, who — along with several other people — has sued Service Corporation International (SCI), "North America's largest single provider of funeral, cremation and cemetery services,"[98] alleging fraudulent and unethical practices. The charges include that "human remains in the care of SCI were misidentified, mistakenly incinerated or disfigured."

> Carroll claims her father's death certificate and cremated remains were mistakenly given to someone outside the family and that her sister's name was forged on a form saying her father had been properly identified.
>
> Carroll says SCI has admitted the forgery, but she and her sister still have no way of knowing if the body SCI cremated was their father's.

After discussing more cases of scandal and fraud, the AARP article outlines the difficulty in compliance. Furthermore,

> at least a dozen states have no meaningful monitoring laws at all. As many as 23 states have "comprehensive" laws, but experts question how protective they really are ... [Finally,] budget cuts are likely to hamper some states in strengthening crematory laws.

Sometimes, accidents happen as well. One postal worker wrote to Ann Landers:

> We see a lot of those cardboard boxes come in for burial at the cemetery. Most of the boxes are not very

---

a murderer to try to destroy a body by cremating it. It would be especially practical if one family member murdered another ..." (Rosen, *Cremation in America*, 156). Dr. Russell Smith, Principal Criminologist at the respected Australian Institute of Criminology, wrote to me in a personal e-mail on July 8, 2009: "Certainly, to assist with forensic procedures burial is preferred."

98 Service Corporation International, http://www.sci-corp.com/SCICORP/home.aspx.

sturdy, nor are they well-sealed. It is not uncommon for us to handle several boxes a week that were so poorly wrapped they were almost empty.[99]

When one such box arrived nearly empty, a supervisor said that he would "just go home and clean out the fireplace" to refill the box."[100]

Of course, the majority of cremations are performed without scandal or incident. But buyer beware — whose ashes are you actually receiving?

---

99 Iserson, *Death to Dust,* 267.
100 Ibid.

-11-

Cost Factors

At one time, the expense of the burial was harder to bear for the family of the deceased than the death itself, so that sometimes they fled to escape the expense.

This was so until the preeminent Jewish leader of the time, Rabbi Gamaliel, insisted that his own body be buried in a plain linen shroud instead of costly garments. And since then we follow the principle of burial in a simple manner.[101]

Some people choose cremation without considering money at all. For others, saving money is their primary consideration.[102]

---

101 Babylonian Talmud, Tractates *Moed Katan* 27b and *Ketubot* 8b.
102 "Perhaps the main motivation is that cremation is much cheaper; there is no casket to purchase, no grave to choose. But people are reluctant to give such a crass reason and so they offer nobler-sounding explanations. They tell you that there will eventually be a shortage of space in the world and so it is better not to have cemeteries. They tell you that cremation is quick and simple and less painful than burial in the earth" (Rabbi Elie Spitz, "Why Bury?" in *Wrestling with the Angel*, ed. Rabbi Jack Riemer [New York: Schocken, 1995], 124–125).

For many, saving money is but one part of a complicated decision-making process.

That being said, as a phenomenon, there is little doubt that *one* of the major factors motivating people to choose cremation in recent years is the issue of cost.

And, in many cases, cremations *are* cheaper than funerals. Many American burials today can cost between $7,000 and $10,000, while the cheapest options for cremation can cost somewhere between $1,000 and $2,000. In hard economic times, that is a significant difference.

When all the associated costs are factored in, however, for most people, the cost difference between cremation and burial is much, much smaller:

> Generally speaking, cremation costs less than traditional burial services … However, there is wide variation in the cost of cremation services, having mainly to do with the amount of service desired by the deceased or the family. A cremation can take place after a full traditional funeral service, which may add cost. The type of container used may also influence cost.[103]

Let us look at the costs of a typical American funeral.[104]

---

103 *New World Encyclopedia*, s.v. "Cremation," http://www.newworldencyclopedia.org/entry/Cremation.

104 These numbers are based on a careful informal survey of a number of average funeral homes around the United Sates. Look online for estimates in your community.

Cost Factors

High-End Burial		High-End Cremation	
Memorial Platinum Funeral Service		*Memorial Platinum Cremation Service*	
The Service		*The Service*	
Minimum services of funeral director and staff	$1,950.00	Minimum services of funeral director and staff	$1,950.00
Embalming*	$695.00	Embalming*	$695.00
Dressing and casketing of deceased	$200.00	Dressing and casketing of deceased	$200.00
Use of facilities — services for visitation	$245.00	Use of facilities — services for visitation	$245.00
Transfer of remains from place of death to funeral home	$595.00	Transfer of remains from place of death to funeral home	$595.00
Funeral vehicle	$345.00	Crematory	$275.00
Limousine	$395.00	Limousine	$395.00
Service vehicle	$195.00	Service vehicle	$195.00
24-hour compassion helpline	$95.00	24-hour compassion helpline	$95.00
Legal plan membership	$150.00	Legal plan membership	$150.00
Flowers	$1,295.00	Flowers	$995.00
Keepsake book	$50.00	Keepsake book	$50.00
Internet memorial	$445.00	Internet memorial	$445.00
Planner	$245.00	Planner	$245.00

* Note that embalming and metal caskets are contrary to Jewish tradition.

Choose one of the following: (1) use of facilities — funeral service in our chapel; (2) staff services — funeral service at other facility; (3) equipment and staff services for "graveside" service	$495.00	Choose one of the following: (1) use of facilities — funeral service in our chapel; (2) staff services — funeral service at other facility; (3) equipment and staff services for "graveside" service	$495.00
The Casket		*The Casket / Memorial Urn Selection*	
____ Rose Stainless Steel Casket with Painted Rose Exterior, Drawer, Panel, Plaque Included ____ Sand Stainless Steel with Brushed Exterior… ____ Silver Sapphire Stainless Steel… ____ Kemper Oak…	$2,795.00	____ Cherry Dark Exterior with Handles	$2,995.00
		____ Bowl Urn ____ Silver Vase Urn ____ Stainless Bronze	$295.00
		____ Heart Urn	$54.00
The Memorial Package		*The Memorial Package*	
Platinum Memorial Package	$595.00	Platinum Memorial Package	$595.00
Totals		*Totals*	
Total Plan Price	$10,785.00	Total Plan Price	$10,964.00
Plan Savings	$890.00	Plan Savings	$1,669.00
Plan Price with Savings	$9,895.00	Plan Price with Savings	$9,295.00

The differences, then, between a first-class burial and a first-class cremation are relatively minor — a difference of $600, or roughly 6 percent. What about those who choose more modest packages?

Burial Packages		Cremation Packages	
Platinum Funeral Service	$9,895.00	Platinum Cremation Service	$9,295.00
Patriot Funeral Service	$9,795.00	n/a	
Heritage Funeral Service	$9,195.00	Heritage Cremation Service	$6,595.00
Value Funeral Service	$7,895.00	Value Cremation Service	$3,995.00
Tribute Funeral Service	$6,795.00	Tribute Cremation Service	$3,295.00
Graveside Service	$4,837.50	n/a	
Immediate Burial*	$2,095.00	Direct Cremation**	$1,820.00

*   With no ceremonies at funeral home, graveside, or anywhere else.
** With no ceremonies at funeral home, graveside, or anywhere else.

Typical savings upon choosing cremation in these scenarios range from $500 to $3,500. Often, there are no savings at all:

> Sheri Richardson Stahl, director of Island Funeral Home in Beaufort, S.C., explained that, "Plenty of times, cremations are just as expensive as burials."[105]

While each case is different, what emerges from all this is that (1) cremations are sometimes cheaper than burials, but not always; and (2) even when cremations are cheaper,[106] the difference is usually not as great as some imagine.

---

105   Molly Kardares, "Another Sign of the Recession — Cremation on the Rise," *CBS News*, March 20, 2009, http://www.cbsnews.com/blogs/2009/03/20/business/econwatch/entry4879269.shtml.
106   The cremation industry has had a complicated relationship with their low-cost reputation. They love the fact that it brings in new customers. But, at first, they didn't quite

Is Cost-Savings behind Cremation?

Considering the lack of significant savings in most cases, it is no wonder that cost is often *not* the primary reason people are choosing cremation. Perhaps the most visible proponent of cremation in America over the last decades is Jack Springer, former head of CANA, the Cremation Association of North America. He explained that

> cremation in the 1990s had "nothing to do with what you spend" ... The typical cremation customer was affluent, not poor, and more than willing to spend money to see loved ones go out in style.[107]

Popular cremation choices over the last decades seem to validate this view. People are sending remains into space, shooting them in fireworks, placing them in concrete coral reefs on the ocean floor,

---

know how to make cremations profitable. Interestingly, over one hundred years ago, in 1874, the *New York Daily Graphic* predicted that there would be money in cremation: "The undertakers to a man / Should favor the cremation plan / Because the more they have to burn / 'Tis evident, the more they'll urn" (Prothero, *Purified by Fire*, 193).

In modern times, funeral directors have used the slogan, "Make money the modern way, Urn it!" (ibid.). By now, cremation is a billion-dollar industry. While some cemetery owners still feel that cremation cuts into their profits, the truth is often otherwise. As one industry publication put it, "We realize some people look at the increase in cremation as a bad thing for cemeteries, but we think this is an exciting time to be a cemeterian" (Tom Smith and Tom Pfeifer, "Cremation and Creativity," *ICFM Magazine*, November 2005, http://www.iccfa.com/reading/2000-2009/cremation-and-creativity).

Interestingly, some cremationists call their businesses "Societies," allowing for the subtle suggestion that they are not-for-profit care organizations out to save you money. These societies are rarely if ever nonprofit. Industry experts explain that the public believes cremation to be low cost, because of many articles in the press emphasizing that point. Since most people want various forms of memorialization and other services, plenty of money is to be made by cremation (see Julie A. Burn, "There's Still Time to Inform Our Customers about Cremation," International Cemetery, Cremation and Funeral Association, April 1, 2009, http://www.iccfa.com/cremation/support/theres-still-time-inform-our-customers-about-cremation).

107 Prothero, *Purified by Fire*, 199.

and turning them into diamonds and other gems, among other options. Scattering ashes from a plane or in the sea is increasingly popular, and also adds significant costs. These options are far from cheap, and business is booming — in these cases, the money factor is not the reason people choose cremation, because the difference in cost is not significant, if it exists at all.

Lowering Funeral Costs

While burial costs *are* often too high, by spending a few minutes thinking it through now (instead of being guilted into quick decisions[108] in the midst of tragedy), these costs can come *way* down:[109]

1. Funeral homes make huge profits on caskets.[110] There is simply no need for an expensive casket. Even the best of them don't prevent natural decomposition, only slightly delay it. If the funeral home is only offering expensive caskets, go to Costco and buy your own — by law, the funeral home must accept it. A simple pine or other wood casket is respectful and dignified.[111]

---

108 For example: "Well, our simplest option is cheaper, but most families like yourselves choose a more respectable send-off for their beloved, such as *silver or gold* …"
109 It also harkens back to how funerals always were, and are supposed to be: "The funeral industry has taken to calling this final undertaking the 'traditional' American funeral service, to suggest that its many ministrations on behalf of the dead are in keeping with a long and honorable history that's worthy of continuing. In fact, today's typical funeral is but a modern construct, and one that bears little resemblance to the way earlier generations cared for, paid tribute to, and buried their dead … [In olden times] there was no vault or coffin hermetically sealed against the elements. No chemical embalming of the remains. A body consigned to the earth would return to the earth and, shortly thereafter, decay and become part of it" (Harris, *Grave Matters*, 41–42).
110 Memorial Society Fund, *How Much Will My Funeral Cost?* (Hinesburg, VT: Funeral and Memorial Societies of America, Inc.). Most funeral home caskets have high markups.
111 As Ernest Morgan put it, "Things like metal burial vaults and caskets with innerspring mattresses make about as much sense as a fur-lined bathtub, but they help wonderfully in running up the bill!" (Iserson, *Death to Dust*, 469). Furthermore, metal caskets

2. Find out if your locality requires concrete liners. Most don't.

3. There is no need to spend $1,000 on flowers. The service can be loving and respectful with no or few flowers.[112]

4. Embalming, which initially became popular in America during the Civil War in order to enable bodies to be shipped home, is today almost always an unnecessary and violent intrusion of the deceased's body. Refrigeration works fine, and the body will not decompose in the first days after death — it will just be paler. Closed caskets are also extremely respectful of the privacy of the deceased.[113]

5. Shop around for funeral homes. Ninety-five percent of people only contact one funeral home![114] This is a mistake, as prices can vary widely.

6. Ask your local rabbi and chevra kadisha (burial society) for ideas on how to get costs down in order to facilitate burial rather than cremation.

By choosing options carefully and making decisions early rather than under the gun, funeral costs can decrease significantly, largely negating the often-quoted cost advantage of cremation.

Direct Cremations

There is one type of cremation whose costs can't be beat: direct cremation. In this type of cremation, a cremation company is con-

---

are against Jewish tradition and philosophy, which values allowing the body to gently return to the earth, not be artificially separated from it.

112 Note that flowers at a funeral are not a Jewish custom.

113 Viewing the body is itself a recent phenomenon, encouraged by the industry ... in order to require the profitable business of embalming. The Jewish tradition frowns on viewing — our loved ones should be remembered for how they looked when they were alive, not dead. Embalming is also against Jewish law.

114 *Market Facts: Report on the Survey of Recent Funeral Arrangers* (Washington, D.C.: Federal Trade Commission, 1988), II:3–4, quoted in Iserson, *Death to Dust*, 480.

tacted online or by telephone. They send someone to pick up the body, deliver it to the crematorium, and deliver to the bereaved family a small can[115] full of cremated remains. Costs are often between $1,000 and $2,000. While it is possible to conduct a parallel "immediate burial," doing so is not always possible, and has never been socially accepted. In an age of worldwide economic difficulty, direct cremations are becoming more common. That is unfortunate.

Here is why:

For some things in life, it is certainly appropriate to find the cheapest solution possible. Times are tough, and we need to live within our means. Why waste money on things that really don't matter?

However, for some life decisions we manage to find the money to do the right thing. For example, I will do whatever is necessary to send my children to a decent school, rather than "going cheap" and putting them in a bad environment. If a loved one needs a medical procedure, I will somehow arrange to make it possible. If I am Jewish and live far away from a Jewish community, I will arrange for a *brit milah* (circumcision) even if I need to pay for a *mohel* (circumciser) to come into town, or I will travel to where it can be done properly.

The point is that cremation usually isn't much cheaper than burial. And even when the difference *is* significant, final decisions about death are *not* the time to go cheap.

Burial *does* matter. It gives the body a permanent and respectful home. It is central to Judaism and monotheistic belief. In our final decision on the planet, it declares calm acceptance of God's will rather than a violent assertion of control. As we will soon see, burial is better for the environment — and for the soul.

Burial is the right decision — and a permanent one. Even when it costs more, we should find ways to make it possible — and do the right thing.

---

115 Or an urn, if you pay extra.

Summary of Part 2

- While decomposition is not pleasant to contemplate, cremation is no better — and possibly much, much worse. Bodies cackle, move, and burn for over two hours, materials are separated by hand, and the bones are then ground up, with some residue from the casket, oven walls, and others' remains being mixed in.
- Modern mobility makes visiting gravesites harder, but burial was never about visitation. Furthermore, within a generation or two, urns will not be lovingly kept. How many urns can a person hold through how many moves? They usually end up discarded without proper respect — better to provide a permanent resting place now.
- While there have been burial scandals, the cremation industry has been rocked by lax or no standards and the nagging question: Since ashes are indistinguishable from one another, how do you know you are receiving the right ones?
- Saving money is a prime factor in many people's decision to choose cremation.
- However, people often compare the most expensive burials to the cheapest cremations. In reality, high-end cremations cost the same as — or close to — high-end burials. Comparing apples to apples and oranges to oranges, cost savings are, in most cases, minor — if they exist at all. Furthermore, with a little planning, funeral expenses can be brought *way* down. While direct cremations are cheaper, we invest more when differences matter, like finding a decent school for our kids. Burial is worth the extra cost.

Part 3
Environmental Concerns

Introduction to Part 3

Many American burials are highly problematic in environmental terms. Over 180,544,000 pounds (81,893,381 kilograms) of steel and 5,400,000 pounds (2,449,398 kilograms) of copper and bronze from metal caskets are put into the ground each year in American cemeteries.[116] In a *Slate* article from 2006, the founder of the Green Burial Council estimated that Americans bury more metal each year than was used to make the Golden Gate Bridge and enough concrete to build a two-lane highway from New York to Detroit.[117]

The cremation industry points out that cremation avoids this high use of resources as well as the environmental evils of embalming: Many studies have found that "embalmers and funeral directors exhibit a higher incidence of leukemia and cancers of the

---

116 Joelle Novey, "Greening Your Final Arrangements," *Green American*, July/August 2008, http://www.greenamerica.org/livinggreen/greenburial.cfm.

117 Nina Rastogi, "The Green Hereafter," *Slate Magazine*, February 17, 2009, http://www.slate.com/id/2211395. Statistics are consistent with those of the Casket and Funeral Association of America, the Cremation Association of North America, Doric Inc., the Rainforest Action Network, and Mary Woodsen, vice president of the Pre-Posthumous Society.

brain and colon ... Agents[118] in embalming compounds pose ... additional health risks."[119] Furthermore, more than 120 gallons of untreated "funeral waste" go directly into the sink per embalming, meaning 827,060 gallons of embalming[120] fluid (including carcinogenic formaldehyde[121]) go into the ground each year.

Many people choose cremation because they believe it is better for the environment. However, as we will see, this is simply not true. Burial is *the* choice of the green movement.

---

118 "Today, a large group of chemical products are made available to perform the [embalming] process. These products are used as arterial fluids, cavity fluids, co-injection fluids, non-arterial preservatives (powders, gels, cauterants, aerosols, and creams), supplement products (solvents, sealants, adhesives), cosmetic products, cleaning compounds (cleansers, soaps, antiseptics, disinfectants, deodorizers) and other miscellaneous products (tissue builders, feature builders, etc.). For this study, about 600 different products were identified" (National Funeral Directors Association, *Funeral Home Wastestream Audit Report*, 1995).
119 Harris, *Grave Matters*, 41.
120 In the standard embalming procedure, blood is drained from the body and replaced with chemicals, lengthening the physical preservation of the body.
121 "EPA regulates formaldehyde as a hazardous waste, yet every embalming includes over three pounds of it each burial" (Harris, *Grave Matters*, 40).

-12-

Land Is for the Living

Cemeteries have always been widely and mistakenly regarded as land wasted on the dead. A frequent argument one hears in favor of cremation relies on the notion, an outright fiction, that we are running out of land. But no one complains about the proliferation of golf courses. We've had three opened in Milford in the last year alone. And no one in public office or private conversation has said that folks should take up contract bridge or ping pong or other less land-needy, acreage-intensive pastimes and dedicate the land, instead, to low-cost housing or co-op organic gardens. No, the development of a golf course is good news to the real estate and construction trades, reason for rejoicing among the hoteliers, restaurateurs, clothiers, and adjoining industries who have found that our species is quite willing to spend money on pleasure when the pleasure is theirs. Land dedicated to the memorialization of the dead is always suspect in a way that land used for recreation of the living seldom is. There seems to be, in my lifetime, an inverse relationship between the size of the TV screen and the space we allow for the dead in our lives and landscapes … We've flattened the tombstones, shortened the services, opted for more and more cremation to keep from running out of land better used for amusement parks, off-street parking, go cart tracks, and golf courses … Less, we seem to be telling the dead, is more; while for the living, enough is never quite enough.[122]

Walmart

In 2009, there were 7,953 Walmart stores around the world, including 3,685 international retail units and 4,268 American retail units.[123] The stores, like the Walmart empire, are enormous. The size of an average Walmart Discount Store is 107,000 square feet (9,941 square meters), while the more common[124] Supercenters each measure 187,000 square feet (17,372 square meters).

In total, the stores already take up over one billion square feet,[125] with between 20 and 22 million square feet (1,858,061–2,043,867

---

122 Lynch, *The Undertaking*, 93.
123 Of these, about 880 were Walmart Stores, 2,630 were Walmart Supercenters, 600 were Sam's Clubs, and the other 150 were neighborhood markets and other stores. In total, Walmart Stores serve customers "more than 200 million times per week … in 15 countries. With fiscal year 2009 sales of $401 billion, Walmart employs almost 2.2 million associates worldwide" ("Walmart Offers $99 Walmart Family Track Pack, NASCAR Driver Appearances and Events for Racing Fans in Atlanta," Walmart Corporate Press Room, http://walmartstores.com/pressroom/news/10694.aspx).
124 Comprising over 60 percent of the total number of stores, a percentage constantly growing.
125 The American stores themselves account for over 640,000,000 square feet and the international stores account for over 500,000,000 square feet, for a total combined square footage of well over 1 billion square feet. According to Walmartfacts.com

square meters) to be added yearly in the United States, and another 26 to 30 million[126] (2,415,479–2,787,091 square meters) to be added internationally.

Note that the sizes mentioned refer only to the size of the stores themselves. It does not include access roads, grass, distribution centers, and delivery areas. In judging total area taken by Walmart, the biggest area to add to the calculation is, by far, parking. Having enough room for cars to park is basic to Walmart's success. A typical Walmart has at least one thousand[127] parking spaces,[128] and very possibly more. This means, in simple terms, that Walmart *already* created well over 4 *million* parking spaces in its 4,268 US stores alone, and is adding 350,000 new spaces in the United States

---

(owned and operated by Walmart), the company continues to grow quickly, adding over 350 US stores per year (and more than that internationally), keeping up with its annual square-footage growth rate of 8 percent.

126 The Walmart website offers an amazing video of the growth of Walmart from 1962 to 2010. See "Watch the Growth of Walmart and Sam's Club," http://projects.flowingdata.com/walmart/. The site reports: "At the end of fiscal year 2010 Walmart has over 4,300 stores and clubs in the U.S., and more than 8,400 units worldwide" (http://investors.walmartstores.com/phoenix.zhtml?c=112761&p=irol-faq). In "Walmart Updates Growth Plans," we are told: "Walmart expects to increase global square footage by approximately 37 million square feet in fiscal year 2011" (http://investors.walmartstores.com/phoenix.zhtml?c=112761&p=irol-newsArticle&ID=1345359&highlight).

Finally, in March 2011, the *Wall Street Journal* reported that Walmart plans to add hundreds of smaller stores to their chain (Miguel Bustillo, "Wal-Mart to Expand 'Express,'" *Wall Street Journal*, March 11, 2011, http://online.wsj.com/article/SB10001424052748704823004576192730258339252.html).

127 Some claim the number is far higher when looked at nationally: "Accommodating up to 2,000 parking spaces on an average" (J. R. Roberts, "Target: Walmart," J. R. Roberts Security Strategies, http://www.jrrobertssecurity.com/articles/wal-mart-parking-lot-crime.htm), and "While a Walmart Supercenter may cover several acres, its parking lot can be three times the size of the store itself, placing its footprint at well over 18 acres" ("A Greener Walmart? Not in Its Parking Lots," WalmartWatch.org, September 25, 2007, http://walmartwatch.org/blog/archives/a_greener_wal_mart_not_in_its_parking_lots/).

128 "Swansea, MA: Wal-Mart Forced to Shrink Its Parking Lot," WalmartWatch.org, http://walmartwatch.org/battlemart/archives/swansea_ma_wal_mart_forced_to_shrink_its_parking_lot/ (accessed October 15, 2010). See also "Wal-Mart Parking Lot Puts Municipal Parking Lot out of Business," *The Onion*, February 8, 2006, http://www.theonion.com/content/node/45118.

to accommodate its 350 new stores — each and every year (international units would double this number).[129]

This means that Walmart, in the United States alone, takes up almost 1.5 *billion* square feet — just for parking (139,354,560 square meters)![130] Its American division adds another 113,750,000 square feet (10,567,721 square meters) for parking — each year.

In essence, including parking and service areas, each Superstore uses up at least 500,000 square feet (46,451 square meters) of space overall.

Compare this to cemeteries. One grave, including space between graves and access paths, takes up about 40 square feet (3.7 square meters). This means that *one* Walmart Superstore can fit well over 12,000 graves.

Approximately 2.6 million Americans die every year.[131] This means that even if every American who died would be buried — and an increasing number are not — the total area taken would

---

[129] How much space do these parking spaces take? Take, for example, a popular midsize car, the Honda four-door 2007 Accord Sedan. Its length is 191.1 inches (485.4 centimeters) or 15.9 feet and its width is 71.6 inches (181.9 centimeters) or 5.967 feet. The Accord's square footage is therefore 94.869 square feet. However, parking spaces need to be slightly bigger than the cars themselves in order to enable one to go in and out. Furthermore, they require driving lanes, dividers, safety embankments, access roads, and more to enable their use. A conservative estimate would suggest that a single parking space averages 9 feet by 19 feet ("A Greener Walmart?" WalmartWatch.org, September 25, 2007).

This corresponds to national averages: The MUTCD (*Manual on Uniform Traffic Control Devices*), the nationwide standard, states that minimal parking spaces are 8 feet by 22 feet and 8 feet by 20 feet for compact vehicles, except on the ends. The end spaces in a line may be as short as 18 feet, or 171 square feet. When circulation areas, driving lanes between each double row of cars, and dividers are added in, parking lots require more space for cars to get to the parking spots than the actual parking spots take! Averaged out, the average parking space requires "about 325 square feet" (roughly 30 square meters). See Wikipedia, s.v. "Parking Space," http://en.wikipedia.org/wiki/Parking_space.

[130] As follows: 4,268 stores multiplied by 1,000 parking spots each multiplied by 325 square feet per space (including driving lanes in parking lot) adds up to 1,387,100,000.

[131] Death rate is 8.4 per 1,000 people. Overall American population (in 2010, as per the U.S. Census Bureau, http://www.census.gov) is about 308 million.

still add up to only 216.7 new Walmart Superstores per year — far less Walmart stores than are actually built.

Jews compromise about 1.5 percent of the American population, and the percentage of Jews among the yearly dead is obviously a very small percentage of the total — and insignificant in terms of space.

The point here is *not* to knock Walmart. The point is that when people claim that "land is for the living" or "there isn't enough land to go around," we need some perspective: How much land are we actually talking about? Of course, land is for the living, but is there *any* room for the dead? And how much comparable land do we, "the living," use for things that, perhaps, we could happily survive without?

Note also that until now we've only discussed Walmart. We haven't listed Lowe's, Home Depot, Target, Costco, shopping malls, and mega malls, or any big-box stores. Combined, their yearly expansion dwarfs that of Walmart. Why are we so quick to refuse a small amount of land for the dead when we happily allow much greater amounts of land for constant development? Is something a little out of balance in the "Land Is for the Living" claim?

And what about golf,[132] NASCAR, and other spectator sports? Amusement parks, casinos, and skiing? Bowling centers? Bars?

---

132 The Golf Research Group reports that there are approximately 32,000 golf courses worldwide, with 59 percent in North America, 19 percent in Europe, 12 percent in Asia, and the other 10 percent scattered around South America, Africa, Australia, and the Middle East. To date, 119 countries have golf courses and well over 50 million people play golf. Between 1990 and 2007, developers built more than 3,000 new golf facilities in the United States, bringing the total to about 16,000. This is half of the world total.

Golf is also booming internationally. In Japan, the number of golf courses before World War II was twenty-three. As of 2008 the number was well over 3,000. Thailand presently has 166 courses *under development!* (*Straits Times*, June 13, 2009). How much space does a golf course take? One writer estimated that "there are roughly ten acres in every par four. Eighteen of those and you have a golf course. Add twenty acres for practice greens, club house, pool and patio, parking and two hundred acres is what you'd need" (Lynch, *The Undertaking*, 86).

Resort areas? Burial is criticized for using up valuable space. The truth is, though, that we use up far, far more space on a wealth of other questionable activities and that, as we will see, there is indeed plenty of room available for burial.

Cremation Gardens

It should be noted, also, that while burials use much less space than people realize, cremation gardens use up land as well. Aside from beautiful gardens and landscaping at the entrance, the typical "plot" size in a cremation garden is about 12 inches by 24 inches (30.5 centimeters by 61 centimeters). One cremation director asked simply:

> Why? Because it's always been like that?
> We decided to create what we call our ledger area, where we allow larger memorials — 30 inches by 48 inches.[133] That provides people with a lot more surface area for etchings, photographs, Biblical verses, favorite poetry. It's very, very popular.[134]

Industry statistics bear this out. The Golf Course Superintendents Association of America states that a typical eighteen-hole golf facility averages about one hundred and fifty to two hundred acres of total land, including water bodies, hard structures, and out-of-play areas (Environmental Institute for Golf, Golf Course Environmental Profile, Golf Course Superintendents Associations of America, 2007, http://www.eifg.org/programs/GCRPfullreport.pdf). This doesn't include parking and access roads, so the total is easily two hundred acres of total land. One acre equals 43,560 square feet, so that each golf course takes over 8,700,000 square feet. Thus, in the United States alone, golf courses cover over 3 million acres of total land, or 139,392,000,000 square feet (that is, over 139 *billion* square feet).

Some environmentalists criticize golf for the huge use of land and the amount of water used. That's not my point. The point here is perspective: It takes only about forty square feet per grave, including walkways. Even if every American who died was buried, it only adds up to about twelve and a half golf courses a year. It would take well over 1,300 years of burial to simply add up to the area we *already* devote to golf courses!

133 That is, 76.2 by 121.9 centimeters.
134 Tom Smith and Tom Pfeifer, "Cremation and Creativity," November 2005.

When one adds in walkways and other service areas, it becomes clear that while cremation does save some space, it is not as big a space-saver as people imagine.

America the Beautiful

The overall surface area of the United States is 3,794,066 square miles (9,826,630 square kilometers).[135] One square mile[136] = 640 acres = 27 million square feet (2,508,382 square meters). Total American deaths are 2.6 million, each taking 40 square feet (3.71 square meters), for a total of 104 million square feet (9,661,916 square meters), which is *less* than 4 square miles (about 10 square kilometers) a year of graves.[137]

Note that these numbers are actually quite high. Jessica Mitford's landmark *The American Way of Death*[138] determined the total number of graves to be 2,842 per acre, meaning that it would take under 1,000 acres (less than 1.5 square miles) a year to bury America's dead.[139]

Considering that the land mass of the United States is over 3,794,066 square miles (9,826,630 square kilometers), even the higher estimate means that every year, new graves add up to one 10,000th of 1 percent of America's area.[140] America would have to be around for another 10,000 years just to add up to 1 percent of our surface area![141] Furthermore, many are surprised to learn how

---

135 *The World Factbook*, s.v. "United States," https://www.cia.gov/library/publications/the-world-factbook/geos/us.html.
136 I.e., 2.59 square kilometers.
137 Four square miles equals one hundred and eight million square feet.
138 New York: Simon & Schuster, 1963.
139 Iserson, *Death to Dust*, 521.
140 The math works out as follows: 100 percent of the land area is about 4 million square miles. Therefore, 10 percent is 400,000 square miles, 1 percent is 40,000 square miles, one 10th of 1 percent is 4,000 square miles, one 100th of 1 percent is 400 square miles, one 1,000th of 1 percent is 40 square miles, and the amount of space we're discussing is one 10,000th of 1 percent, or 4 square miles (even less, as we said!).
141 And, presumably, most present-day cemeteries would not survive 10,000 years.

little of American land is actually "taken up." The United States Department of Agriculture's report, *Major Uses of Land in the United States, 2002,* revealed that

> the United States has a land area of about 2.3 billion acres, which is allocated among a variety of uses ... The largest shares of the Nation's land were allocated to forest use, grassland pasture and range, and cropland ...
>
> About 20 percent[142] of the land area was cropland in 2002, 26 percent was permanent grassland pasture and range, and 29 percent was forest-use land. Urban areas constituted just 3 percent of U.S. land, while a variety of special uses accounted for 13 percent of the land base and miscellaneous other uses comprised the remaining 10 percent.[143]

In other words, the amount of land that cemeteries use is incredibly small. As a person drives through America — or flies in an airplane — he or she sees seemingly unending vast areas of untouched land — much of it only a short distance from urban centers. Much should be preserved and protected. Some can be used for agriculture, development, and other all kinds of human activity. Of course, land is primarily for the living.

But can't 0.0001 percent be devoted to honoring the dead?

---

142   Or 442 million acres.
143   Ruben N. Lubowski, Marlow Vesterby, Shawn Bucholtz, Alba Baez, and Michael J. Roberts, *Major Uses of Land in the United States, 2002/EIB-14* (United States Department of Agriculture: Economic Research Service, May 2006), http://www.ers.usda.gov/publications/eib14/.

-13-

Energy Use

In India, Hindus traditionally perform public, open-air cremations over a wood fire. It takes five to six hours for the body to burn in this manner. Nationwide, Indian cremations destroy over fifty million trees a year — an acknowledged environmental disaster.

Western industrial cremation doesn't use trees. As *Slate Magazine* reports, modern crematories

> don't run on lollipops and puppy dog tails — most use a combination of natural gas and electricity to incinerate their occupants. One leading manufacturer [stated] that a typical machine requires about 2,000 cubic feet of natural gas and 4 kilowatt-hours of electricity per body.[144]

Another writer commented that

---

144   Nina Rastogi, "The Green Hereafter," February 17, 2009.

on the surface, cremation seems like a more friendly and convenient way to deal with the bodily remains of a loved one. But, let's consider the impact of this truly industrial process ... the amount of non-renewable fossil fuel needed to cremate bodies in North America is equivalent to a car making 84 trips to the Moon and back ... each year.[145]

In reviewing cremation's energy use, let us consider some energy facts published by the cremation industry itself.

One of the industry leaders, B & L Cremation Systems, reports the following energy usage of two of its models:

Phoenix II-1		Phoenix II-2	
Maximum input rating	2,000,000 Btu's per hour	Maximum input rating	2,500,000 Btu's per hour
After burner maximum	1,200,000 Btu's per hour	After burner maximum	1,500,000 Btu's per hour
Modulation minimum	100,000	Modulation minimum	100,000
Ignition burner	300,000	Ignition burner	300,000
Cremation burner	500,000	Cremation burner	500,000
		Emission burner	200,000

Many other systems use between 1.2 and 2 or 2.2 million Btu's per hour.[146]

---

[145] Hal Stevens, "Cremation or Burial — Carbon Emissions and the Environment," The Free Library, April 21, 2009, http://www.thefreelibrary.com/Cremation+or+Burial+-+Carbon+Emissions+and+the+Environment-a01073949157.

[146] See the websites of Crawford, B & L, Matthews, and others.

What Is a Btu?

Btu stands for a British thermal unit.[147] In order to compare different types of fuel usage and determine which methods are the most efficient, scientists use a common unit of measurement, the Btu. Some examples:

- A home gas furnace will usually use about 60,000 Btu per hour.[148]
- A pool heater can use at least 200,000 Btu per hour.[149]
- One billion Btu equals all the electricity that 300 households consume per month.

How many Btu's do various fossil fuels actually provide?

- 1 ton of coal provides 20,169,000 Btu.
- 1 cubic foot of natural gas provides 1,028 Btu.
- 1 gallon of gasoline provides 124,000 Btu.[150]
- 1 gallon of diesel and heating oil provides 139,000 Btu.

When the numbers are added up, a startling fact emerges. While one Btu is a very small amount of energy, cremators use well over one million Btu's *an hour* — and an average-sized body takes about two hours to burn.[151]

These numbers reflect what the cremation industry itself claims:

---

[147] Technically, the Btu is the amount of heat required to raise the temperature of 1 pound of liquid water by 1 degree Fahrenheit at the temperature that water has its greatest density (approximately 39 degrees Fahrenheit), which is approximately equal to the energy released in the burning of a wood match.

[148] A free-standing range will often use 40,000 Btu per hour, and an outdoor barbeque grill will use between 25,000 and 30,000 Btu per hour.

[149] A gas dryer will use at least 20,000 Btu/hr.

[150] One barrel of crude oil (equivalent to 42 US gallons) provides 5,800,000 Btu.

[151] Large bodies take longer.

> The average fuel consumption of our systems is 700 to 1,000 cubic feet [of natural gas] per hour.[152]

In other words, *cremations use up an enormous amount of fossil fuels,* which as we know are the single greatest polluters of the environment.

Take two more examples from a different industry leader. One Crawford model, the Elite Cremation System Model C1000H, uses 1,200,000 Btu per hour and uses 12 gallons of LP fuel per hour.[153] Per cremation, this adds up to at least 2,000,000 Btu's used, or about 20 gallons of fuel.

A second Crawford model, the Ultimate Cremation System Model C1000S, estimates 2,100,000 BTU per hour and uses 21 gallons of LP fuel per hour.[154] Per cremation, this adds up to almost 3,000,000 Btu's used, or over 25 gallons of fuel.

---

152 See, for example, B & L Cremation Systems, Inc., http://www.blcremationsystems.com/faq.html. How does this work out? As we saw above, cremators use up well over 1 million (and sometimes 2 million) Btu's per hour. Since one cubic foot of natural gas provides 1,028 Btu's, each hour of cremation will therefore burn up about 1,000 cubic feet of natural gas — and with cremators burning about 100 pounds of flesh per hour, over 2,000 cubic feet of natural gas are burned per cremation.

153 These numbers are taken directly from the maker's brochures, describing fuel use as it relates to actual operating costs:

Crawford Industrial Group, LLC, Predicted Operational Cost Analysis, Elite Cremation System – Model C1000H

Operational Fuel Costs (Fuel Use Assumptions):
- Hours of operation: 8 hours/day, 5 days/week, 260 days/year
- Incinerator outlet temperature: 1600–1800°F
- Auxiliary fuel usage: 1,200,000 Btu/hour
- Cost per gallon of LP fuel: $2.50/gallon

Fuel Use Calculations: 1,200,000 Btu per hr (divided by 1,000 Btu/FT3 = 1,200 CFH Fuel Usage. 1,200 CF/Hr divided by 100 CF / gallon) = 12.00 gallon per hour. Multiply this by $2.50 per gallon and we find that each system uses $30.00 worth of fuel per hour of operation. Add in electrical costs and the total net operating costs equal $30.34 per hour of operation.

154 These numbers are taken directly from the maker's brochures, describing fuel use as it relates to actual operating costs:

Crawford Industrial Group, LLC Predicted Operational Cost Analysis Ultimate Cremation System – Model C1000S

Several other factors should be considered: (1) the obesity epidemic; (2) artificially low industry assessments of actual energy use; (3) additional resource depletion due to the cremation process.

The Obesity Epidemic

Americans are getting fatter, a fact well documented by the media. It takes longer to cremate bigger bodies and therefore more fossil fuels are being used. Most models can burn about one hundred pounds of flesh per hour.[155] As bodies get fatter, more fossil fuels are necessary to burn them.

Actual Energy Use

Consciously or not, industry fuel-efficiency claims are lower — sometimes significantly so — than reality. Their sales literature attempts to convince cemeteries and funeral homes to buy their cremators. One of the biggest selling points is how "little" energy is used compared to competitors' models — translating into lower

---

Operational Fuel Costs (Fuel Use Assumptions):
- Hours of operation: 8 hours/day, 5 days/week, 260 days/year
- Incinerator outlet temperature 1600°F–1800°F
- Average waste stream fuel content 1,000 Btu / pound
- Average auxiliary fuel usage 1,200,000 Btu / hour. Cost per gallon of LP fuel: $2.50/gallon

Fuel Use Calculations: 2,100,000 Btu / hr (divided by 1000 Btu/FT3 = 2,100 CFH Fuel Usage. 2,100 CF/Hr divided by 100 CF/gallon) which equals 21.00 gallon per hour of use, multiplied by $2.50/gallon equals $52.50 for fuel per hour of operation. Add in the electrical costs and the Total Net Operating Costs: $52.54 per hour of operation.

[155] "Obese cases take longer than regular cremations due to the amount of material that is being cremated and with large amounts of fat being present, the unit is operated slower to better control the combustion process … Most of our models operate at an average 100 pounds per hour destruction rate …" (B & L Cremation Systems, Inc., "Crematory & Incinerator Frequently Asked Questions," http://www.blcremationsystems.com/FAQCremation.html).

fuel costs for the bottom line. Several cremation operators themselves told me, off the record, that actual energy use was far higher than expected. They don't complain about this publicly because even with added energy costs, their profit margins are still very high. Furthermore, operators benefit tremendously from the eco-friendly label that many customers mistakenly assume they have — no need to rock the boat and get people thinking about the reality of cremation's energy use.

One manufacturer publicly admitted:

> When a customer makes a choice to purchase a crematory, probably the most important feature is fuel consumption, because it relates to the bottom line every time you operate your equipment. No other cremation function will have such a sizeable effect on your operation. It seems that each manufacturer states they have the lowest fuel consumption and the fuel data they have provided you with is not really what the equipment uses.[156]

Additional Resource Depletion

Actual fuel burned in the process is the largest user of natural resources, but not the only one. Urns manufactured of rare woods, bronze, and steel are resource intensive and can cause considerable pollution. The cremators themselves are massive industrial ovens, requiring an enormous amount of energy and metal to produce. The catalog of equipment necessary for a cremation operation is full of items such as processing stations, stainless steel funnels, stands, urn loaders, body trays, pacemaker detectors, hand trigger magnets, cremation chamber brushes, temporary containers, aluminized clothing, full- and half-face respirators, aluminum and

---

156 B & L information packet received in May 2009, "Fuel Efficiency."

other types of gloves, face shields, refractory lined stacks, over fifty types of spare parts, infant cremation pans, and hydraulic scissors. Cremators also use at least four kilowatts of electricity per hour of operation, in addition to natural gas. Finally,

> scatterings at sea often occur on large boats, with many families, belching diesel fuel and smoke into the ocean.[157]

Environmentalists claim that when all these factors are added:

Cremation requires energy for complete combustion. A lot of energy.[158]

The overall American percentage of deaths being followed by cremation is quickly approaching 40 percent.[159] With 2.6 million deaths per year, that means approximately 1.04 million cremations occur in the United States yearly[160] — an enormous use of fossil fuels.

---

157 Green Cremations, http://www.green-cremations.com/Cremation%20Info.htm (accessed August 24, 2009).
158 Ibid.
159 Funeral Consumers Alliance of North Texas, "Cremation — What Are the Rates in the U.S.?" http://fcant.org/index.php?option=com_content&view=article&id=255:what-are-the-cremation-rates-in-the-us&catid=41:Check%20here%20for%20answers%20first&Itemid=57.
160 A typical cremator today uses over 1 million Btu per hour with an average cremation lasting between one and a half and two hours, sometimes more. A conservative estimate of Btu's per cremation, then, is a minimum of 1.5 million each. Cremations nationally are already consuming over 1.5 million million, or 1.5 trillion, Btu's per year. It may help to visualize this: 1,000,000 = 1 million. 1,000,000,000 = 1 billion. 1,000,000,000,000 = 1 trillion. Cremations account for 1,500,000,000,000 Btu's every year in the United States alone.

-14-

Toxic Emissions

Environmentalists are also very concerned about cremation's toxic emissions:

> Scrubbers, filters, and after-chambers can reduce but not entirely eliminate the raft of pollutants generated by the incineration of a human body. Carbon monoxide (a common product of combustion) and fine soot comprise the primary emissions, but sulfur dioxide (from combustion of the natural gas fuelant) and trace metals (from body parts, among others) may also be produced.
>
> Of all emissions, however, mercury poses the biggest threat to the health of the living. The toxic metal, which is linked to brain and neurological damage in children, is found in dental amalgams.
>
> The cremation retort's high temps vaporize any mercury in dental fillings of the deceased, sending the metal up the stack and into the atmosphere. From

there it's carried by prevailing winds, some of it falling into lakes and streams, where it's taken up by fish and other aquatic life — and eventually by humans who consume them.[161]

Much has been written about the high volume of toxic emissions from cremation. The cremation industry claims that new technologies have vastly improved the situation. While there has indeed been some improvement, new cremators still produce disturbingly high amounts of dangerous emissions. And, of course, the vast majority of cremation ovens in operation don't even have the new technologies — "more than 80 percent of crematories in the U.S. do NOT use environmentally friendly practices."[162] Cremators point out that they comply with environmental standards. This may be true, technically: In most places, the standards are weak or nonexistent.

The Reindl Study

Articles about the environmental effects of cremation often refer to the 2008[163] analysis[164] of John Reindl from the Department of Public Works of Dane County, Wisconsin. He collected available data on mercury emissions and concluded that on average, *each human cremation* releases between 2.0 and 3.0 grams of mercury

---

161 Harris, *Grave Matters*, 61.
162 Green Cremations, http://www.green-cremations.com/Cremation%20Info.htm (accessed August 24, 2009).
163 It should be noted that the dangers have been known for a long time: "The increasing use of cremation could lead to problems in view of the thermal instability of mercury alloys, the volatility of the free metal, its cumulative toxicity, and the aggregate amounts now involved" (Alan Mills, "Mercury and Crematorium Chimneys," *Nature*, August 16, 1990, 615).
164 *Summary of References on Mercury Emissions from Crematoria,* November 3, 2008, http://www.ejnet.org/crematoria/reindl.pdf.

into the atmosphere, "which is a significant source of this type of pollution."[165]

The EPA estimated that, in 2005, cremations produced about 3,000 *kilograms* of mercury which was subsequently released into air, the third largest source of mercury from any products in the country. In the United Kingdom, estimates vary on the percentage of mercury emissions resulting from cremations, ranging from 11 percent to 35 percent. The Swedish Environmental Protection Agency estimated in 2001 that cremations accounted for 32 percent of mercury emissions to the atmosphere in that country.[166] A Canadian report from 2001 estimated that its crematories were putting about 120 kilograms of mercury a year into the atmosphere, based on 1995 numbers. Reindl emphasizes that few studies exist in North America and that there are significant uncertainties as to the actual effects. He comments that no known standards for cremation emissions exist, so it is difficult to ascertain how bad the situation really is.[167]

The British Columbia Study

A recent study[168] from British Columbia, Canada, added much to scientific knowledge and debate about mercury and other cremation emissions.

The study noted that, like most other jurisdictions, "there are no legal requirements for emission control for crematoria in British Columbia" and pointed out the following:

- Emissions from crematoria include pollutants such as particulate matter, volatile organic compounds,

---
165 Pioneer Burials, http://www.pioneerburials.com/article_info.php?articles_id=2 (accessed September 1, 2009).
166 Reindl, *Mercury Emissions from Crematoria*, November 3, 2008.
167 Ibid.
168 Veerle Willaeys, *Public Health Impact of Crematoria*, Memorial Society of British Columbia, http://www.memorialsocietybc.org/c/g/cremation-report.html.

carbon monoxide, nitrogen oxides, sulfur dioxides, hydrogen chloride, heavy metals (cadmium, mercury, and lead), dioxins, and furans.

- Mercury emissions may be significant and disturbing, and are transported long distances.[169] Estimates of average mercury release per cremation of a human body normally vary between three and five grams.[170]

- People living in the vicinity of crematoria are probably more affected by other pollutants such as particulate matter and pollutants from incomplete combustion.

- Mercury has been found to be significantly elevated in the hair of crematorium workers.[171]

- Since cremation burns organic matter, dioxins[172] and

---

[169] "Most Mercury is volatilized as elemental mercury, some is oxidized and a small fraction is bound to particulate matter. Volatilized Mercury re-deposits and may bio-accumulate in the food chain after methylation by microbiota" (ibid.).

[170] According to the National Atmospheric Emissions Inventory (NAEI), it is 3.41 to 5 grams in Sweden and Finland, similar to the 3 gram finding from studies from Mills in United Kingdom and Kunzler and Andree in Switzerland. Emissions from crematoria were estimated to be the third highest emission source of mercury in Sweden (ibid.).

[171] "Especially in administrators who work in closed environment with limited air ventilation. Of the 97 crematoria workers, 3% had concentrations higher than 6 ppm which is considered as the maximum tolerable level. Mean mercury concentrations were 1.96 ppm for administrative personnel and 1.47 ppm for ground personnel compared to 0.97 ppm for controls. The number of amalgam fillings was taken into consideration. A limiting factor of the study is that there is no information on possible diet exposure to mercury. The authors argue that fish is only a minor part in the diet in the UK. The authors conclude that this study contributes to the evidence that emission monitoring and control is warranted" (ibid.).

[172] A dioxin is a "heterocyclic, organic, antiaromatic compound," a dangerous group of compounds including the famous PCDDs, responsible for Vietnam War veteran illnesses, the Seveso disaster, and the poisoning of Viktor Yushchenko (*Wikipedia*, s.v. "Dioxins and Dioxin-Like Compounds," http://en.wikipedia.org/wiki/Dioxins_and_dioxin-like_compounds).

furans[173] are often formed[174] during the process, due to incomplete combustion or new formation in the stack induced by high temperatures.

- Cremations also produce greenhouse gases such as carbon dioxides and nitrogen oxides.

The report shares the following conclusions, among others:

- Crematoria have the potential to have a negative impact on public health.
- There is a lack of emission data of existing facilities in North America. The few emission studies that have been done are on new facilities.
- Internationally, there is clearly a concern around the polluting capacity of crematoria.
- "A crematorium should not be sited close to a neighborhood."

---

173 Furan (also known as furane and furfuran) is a heterocyclic organic compound which is toxic and may be carcinogenic (*Wikipedia*, s.v. "Furans," http://en.wikipedia.org/wiki/Furan).

174 In the United States, the emission of dioxins and furans measured at a crematorium with new technology was 0.5 µg TEQ per cremated body. European test data found higher values: 4.9 µg TEQ per body at two Dutch crematoria and 70–80 µg TEQ in a British crematorium with older technology. Reviewers of the EPA dioxin emission inventory report recommend using the Dutch data as reference. A Japanese study, Takeda et al. (2001), found an average of 3.9 µg and a median of 1.8 µg TEQ/body with a maximum of 24 µg TEQ/ body. The operational condition of the crematorium, mainly the temperature control, influenced to a large extent the emission of dioxins and furans. Takeda found in a study in Japan 1998 measurements ranging from 9.9 pg to 6500 pg TEQ/m3 and in a second study in 2001 measurements between 64 pg TEQ/m3 and 24000 pg TEQ/m 3 (Willaeys, *Public Health Impact*).

Understanding the Mercury Problem

The main source of mercury in human cremations is dental amalgams, the most commonly used material for dental fillings, which contain about 50 percent mercury.

It is a challenge that is not easily solved. Modern scrubbers can reduce the amount of mercury sent into the atmosphere, but they produce waste and ash with the mercury instead. Some suggest physically removing fillings before cremation. Understandably, families usually object to this ghoulish idea. Others suggest adding selenium to the cadaver — when incinerated together a compound is formed that will stick the mercury to the walls of the retort rather than allow it to be released into the atmosphere. However, selenium itself is considered a pollutant and the effects of this solution may be even worse than the problem it is trying to solve — no one yet knows. Finally, others suggest waiting for the mercury problem to eventually solve itself — amalgam's use as dental fillings is on the decline. Perhaps, but the decline is slow and we have many, many decades left of many, many millions of amalgams in people's mouths to deal with.

Because so much mercury is released in cremations, it is important to understand how dangerous the stuff is:

> Exposure to mercury can cause serious illnesses and even death. Children and pregnant women face the greatest risk for adverse health effects. In fact, children exposed to the same dose of mercury as an adult will suffer adverse effects much sooner. Pregnant women are at heightened risk because mercury crosses the placenta and can cause both neurological and cognitive problems to the fetus.[175]

---

175 Pioneer Burials, http://www.pioneerburials.com/article_info.php?articles_id=2 (accessed September 1, 2009).

Health Dangers

Many health studies[176] warn of the dangers of crematoria, including but not limited to the mercury problem:

A 2003 study revealed that "the risk of stillbirth was 4% higher and the risk of the life threatening brain abnormality anencephalus was 5% higher among babies whose mothers lived near to crematoria."[177]

Canada's Interior Health Authority did a literature review and "concluded that fumes from crematoriums are potentially harmful and that they should not be located close to a residential area." It also "found that particulate matter, which can be inhaled deep into lung tissue, is the chief threat."[178]

The EPA's *2000 Inventory of Dioxin Emissions in the United States*[179] estimates that crematoria emit 410 nanograms of dioxin TEQ (toxic equivalents) per body. This equals the amount of dioxin released when burning 3,205 pounds of tires, 320 pounds of trash, or 426 pounds of hazardous waste in a hazardous waste incinerator — for each and every body burned.[180]

Furthermore, many families choose to scatter ashes by boat or plane, or send ashes deep into reefs in the sea, space, or fireworks. Aside from additional use of fossil fuels, all of these options add significantly to pollutant emissions.

The *New World Encyclopedia* reports that

> there exists a body of research that indicates cremation has a significant impact on the environment. Major

---

176 This section is largely based on material from EJNet.org, "Crematoria," http://www.ejnet.org/crematoria/.
177 T. J. B. Dummer, H. O. Dickinson and L. Parker, "Incinerators May Put Babies at Risk," *Journal of Epidemiology and Community Health* 57, May 29, 2003, 456–461.
178 Dr. Perry Kendall, "Put a Lid on Fumes from Cremation," *Vancouver Sun*, May 12, 2006.
179 *The Inventory of Sources and Environmental Releases of Dioxin-Like Compounds in the United States: The Year 2000 Update*, External Review Draft, March 2005.
180 EJNet.org, "Crematoria."

emissions from crematories include nitrogen oxide, carbon monoxide, sulfur dioxide, particulate matter, mercury, hydrogen fluoride, hydrogen chloride, and other heavy metals, in addition to Persistent Organic Pollutants (POP).[181]

Another commentator gave numbers to the effects of operating a cremation oven:

> A typical machine requires about 2,000 cubic feet of natural gas and 4 kilowatt-hours of electricity per body. That means the average cremation produces about 250 pounds of CO_2 equivalent, or about as much as a typical American home generates in six days.[182]

A government report[183] from South Australia concluded that cremation created around 160 kilograms (353 pounds) of carbon dioxide, compared to 39 kilograms of carbon dioxide for each burial. In other words, cremation produces, per body, over four times more carbon dioxide than burial.[184]

---

181 *New World Encyclopedia*, s.v. "Cremation," http://www.newworldencyclopedia.org/entry/Cremation.
182 Rastogi, "The Green Hereafter," February 17, 2009.
183 *Natural Burial Grounds: Sixty-Second Report of the Environment, Resources and Development Committee*, September 24, 2008.
184 Research on the carbon impact of cremation and burial was carried out by a large Australian cemetery, Centennial Park Cemetery in the South Australian state capital of Adelaide, which carries out more than 900 burials and 3,300 cremations a year. Chief executive Bryan Elliott reported that every cremation created around 160 kilograms (353 pounds) of carbon dioxide, compared to 39 kilograms of carbon dioxide for each burial. In other words, over four times more carbon dioxide for cremation. However, Elliott concluded that overall, when the cost of maintaining gravesites, mostly covered by lawns at Centennial Park, is taken into account, cremations came out 10 percent greener than burials.

"This is because we must look after the gravesite for a number of years by watering and mowing the surrounding lawn area and maintaining the concrete beam on which the headstone is placed," Elliott said. "Burial is a more labor and resource intensive process, consumes more fuels, and produces larger quantities of waste than cremation," added Elliott (ibid.).

Conclusions

Emissions and energy use form a classic catch-22 situation. American incinerators generally burn bodies at higher temperatures, using more fossil fuels in the process, but eliminating some toxic emissions (although still emitting far too many). European incinerators burn at a lower temperature, thus using less fossil fuels, but sending even more toxic emissions into the environment.[185] A hard choice to make, since both options are bad for the environment.

We no longer burn leaves or trash because we are aware of the pollutants put into the atmosphere and their harmful effects. As we have seen in many studies, cremations produce significant toxic emissions that are harmful to the environment, both locally and globally. Concerns over enormous use of fossil fuels and high emissions are two of the main reasons that environmentalists do *not* favor cremations.

Since these conclusions seem to go against the widespread environmental opposition to cremation, I investigated further and spoke to Elliott in August of 2009. It seems that his conclusions are often misunderstood and/or misrepresented. First, the method by which he achieved his results is not known or repeatable, the ABCs of scientific research. Second, he writes on his site and repeated clearly on the phone that his cemetery is very unique in its size, greenage, and maintenance needs, and "the numbers may be different" — very different — for others. Furthermore, I believe approaches like this are suspect for several reasons: (1) Cremation memorials, gardens, niches, and trees also have serious maintenance needs; (2) not factored into these equations — at all — are fossil fuel use for sea and air scatterings; (3) same with construction and maintenance of the crematoria ovens themselves; (4) inherent biases towards cremation are perhaps reflected in this nonscientific number crunching. Even after reading his report, environmentalists are not in favor of cremation.

185 For more on this, see Marc Deslauriers, *Emission Inventory Guidebook* (Ottowa, ON: Environment Canada, Criteria Air Contaminants Division, 2006).

-15-
Giving Back to Planet Earth

> At some point the [New Guinea aboriginal tribe the] Fore had recognized that plants grew better in places where bodies were buried, and began planting crops there. The burials [are reminiscent] of the film strips ... in grade school that showed American Indians using fish to fertilize corn crops. For a people considered primitive, the Fore, like Native Americans, had been amazingly astute ... they'd made the connection between death and fertility.[186]

Earth burial actually *helps* the ground. When any living organism dies and returns to the earth, its body itself benefits the earth greatly. As author and environmentalist Mark Harris put it,

---

186 Harris, *Grave Matters*, 162.

> As it decays, the body releases into the surrounding soil its cache of organic nutrients. The microbes, insects, and other organisms that attend a decaying corpse further nourish the ground with their leavings and remains; they also aerate the dirt, loosening compacted earth and thereby creating fertile ground ...[187]

Unfortunately, many modern funerals negate this blessing to the earth through embalming and metal caskets.[188] Embalming is unnecessary in the vast majority of cases today and *not* required by law (refrigeration is more than adequate), and it releases toxic chemicals into the earth. Metal caskets add tons of nonbiodegradable metal into the ground, delaying and negating the positive effects of the body itself.

If one avoids embalming and chooses a simple wooden casket,[189] burial is in fact a blessing to the earth. Decomposition is a positive natural process that *adds* nutrients, health, and fertility to Planet Earth. As one writer puts it,

> To allow, and even invite, the decay of one's physical body — its tissues and bone, its cache of organic components — and return what remains to the very elements it sprang from, as directly and simply as possible ... to give back to the earth some very small measure of the vast resources they drew from it in life and, in the process, perpetuate the cycles of nature, of growth and decay, of death and rebirth, that sustain us all.[190]

---

187 Ibid., 172.
188 Roughly three-quarters of caskets sold today are metal (ibid., 135).
189 Thus following Jewish law, as well.
190 Ibid., 2.

Burn Away the Nutrients?

In a modern cremation, the casket is placed in the retort (the cremation chamber), and the temperature is raised to approximately 1600–1800 degrees Fahrenheit (871–982 degrees Celsius). What is left after cremation?

> After approximately two to two and a half hours, all organic matter is consumed by heat and vaporization. The residue remaining is bone fragments, which are then carefully removed from the cremation chamber.[191]

This last quotation, taken from the National Cremation Society website, is consistent with other descriptions[192]: the whole point of modern cremation is to burn away almost the entire body. The cremation industry prides itself on the efficacy of their burners — nothing is left but bone fragments, which are then scooped up, ground into a fine dust, and presented to the mourners.

While efficient, cremation — by definition — prevents a body's nutrients from enriching the ground.

Plant a seed and growth can occur: When a plant or living organism decomposes, the ground is given new life.

Try burning a seed and then planting it: Growth is impossible. Burnt ashes provide no fertilizer and no growth.

The sprinkling of ashes can actually damage the environment:

> The mountaineering Council of Scotland asked bereaved relatives to avoid the most popular sites on Scottish summits because of worries that the volume of ashes was causing soil changes. In Leicestershire,

---

191 National Cremation Society, "The Cremation Process," http://www.nationalcremation.com/dm20/en_US/main/ncs/information/cremation.page.

192 "After approximately two to two and a half hours, all organic matter is consumed by heat or evaporation" (Richard Rutherford, *Honoring the Dead: Catholics and Cremation Today* [Collegeville, MN: Liturgical Press, 2001], 30).

boaters on the River Soar complained that if mourners continue to sprinkle ashes there, it will become unusable. Similarly conservation officers on Snowdon [Wales' highest mountain] recently asked people to consider alternatives because of the ecological effects on the vegetation. When [the British football team] Manchester City moved from Maine Road to the City of Manchester Stadium they had to build a special memorial garden because demand to scatter ashes was so high, there were worries it would affect the pitch.[193]

While the contents of a single urn being scattered in a forest (assuming no one else uses the same spot) will not cause irreparable damage to the environment, what is happening to the popular sites is an important lesson for all scattering: ashes damage rather than help the environment.

Considering the enormous use of fossil fuels, toxic emissions, and needless destruction of organic nutrients, it is not surprising that mainstream environmentalists are not delighted with modern cremation:

> From a biological point of view, and in consideration of the environment as well, cremation … is not a particularly good alternative … Each cremation takes about 20 litres of fuel oil and half a kilogram of activated carbon … gases, also containing mercury, are released into the air … And this still happens despite extensive measures to reduce emissions.
>
> Burial of the ash can take place in an urn or casket grave at the place of one's choice … But already upon the first rainfall after burial the ash is on its way from

---

193 Emma Cook, "Saying Goodbye Our Way," *Guardian*, August 19, 2006, http://www.guardian.co.uk/lifeandstyle/2006/aug/19/familyandrelationships.family.

the site. It runs with the rainwater and continues to waterways until it ends up in the sea where it worsens eutrophication and oxygen depletion …

Although cremation was promoted after the Second World War as environmentally preferable to burial, modern thinking is challenging this. Gas is consumed in the process and harmful pollutants are released into the atmosphere … Natural decomposition after burial seems less harmful to the environment …[194]

Conclusion

As human beings, our bodies are nourished from the ground. Fruit. Vegetables. Grains. Water. Meat. Directly or indirectly, our bodies live through the nutrients we receive from the ground. Burial is a blessing to our planet, returning our bodies to the land.

Cremation, on the other hand, burns the nutrients and gives nothing back to the planet that gave us so much.

Mainstream environmentalists do not favor cremation. They suggest[195] returning to a purer form of burial. Skipping embalming. Choosing a simple wood or even bamboo coffin (or just shrouds). Finally, they suggest making burial grounds more environmentally friendly. In other words, burning is not the answer to legitimate environmental concerns — simplicity is.

---

194 Promessa: Organic Burial, "Cremation," http://www.promessa.se/facts/cremation/?lang=en.
195 Do an Internet search for "green burial" and see the results.

Summary of Part 3

- Land *is* for the living, but we have far more land than we realize. In the United States, for example, if everyone was buried, it would take 10,000 years to take up 1 percent of our land mass. Jews constitute a negligent amount of this land use. Much of this available land is close to urban centers, and we use far, far more land on frivolous activities. Can't 0.0001 percent of our land be used for the dead?

- Typical American burials *are* bad for the environment. However, this is due to metal caskets and embalming, both of which are against Jewish tradition.

- Cremation uses an enormous amount of electricity (and thus fossil fuels) to burn bodies.

- Cremation also releases many toxic fumes (including mercury) into the atmosphere. While not regulated in the United States, international research recommends that crematoria not be built in residential areas.

- Burying a body helps the earth. Scattering ashes hurts it.

- Cremation is *not* the choice of environmentalists around the world — burial (with no embalming or metal caskets) is.

Part 4
Spiritual Concerns

Introduction to Part 4

We modern people are often uncomfortable talking about spiritual concerns. Many contemporary Jews in particular are reluctant to discuss the soul and the afterlife.

Yet no discussion of burial and cremation can be complete without focusing on the domain of the spirit. What happens after we die? Do our choices regarding death have any effect on what happens next? Is the soul aware of what is happening to its body? Do we know what is happening to it?

In this section, we will delve deeper and explore Jewish concepts surrounding spirituality and the afterlife — and see how they relate to burial and cremation.

-16-
The Soul Is Aware

Who are funerals for, anyway?

It sounds like a silly question, but the answer forms the basis of many decisions made at this sensitive time.

Some believe that decisions made after death — for example, whether to bury or burn, and what type of service to conduct — are for the living. To give a sense of closure. To provide comfort. After all, the dead person is … dead. Whatever we do doesn't matter to him anyway. He is already in a "better place." He doesn't feel what is happening to his body, doesn't really care, and probably isn't even aware anyway. Mourning practices, then, are understood to be for the mourners.

The Jewish view is different. While providing comfort to the bereaved is central to Jewish tradition (and is crucial to mourning practices), it is not the only factor to be considered. The soul of the departed needs to be taken into consideration as well, and some questions (what is done with the body at the time of the funeral, for instance) focus almost exclusively on the soul's needs, rather than on the mourners' needs.

The Body-Soul Connection

A soul is not put in a body randomly. God creates a particular body that suits the challenges of a particular soul as it begins its mission on earth. One soul may need a tall and strong body to fulfill its mission here on earth. Another soul might need to overcome sickness, and is therefore given a weak body. In both cases they are perfect for each other — a match made in Heaven.[196]

The body challenges the soul, of course — will a person control his physical desires or be controlled by them? This struggle is central to who we are and who we will become.

Interestingly, though, in Jewish thought the body and soul are not enemies. The body enables the soul to dwell in this world, to bring meaning into daily life. Without the body, the soul could not fulfill its mission. Body and soul are partners, together for a lifetime.

Since they are partners, the soul becomes attached to its body. When death occurs, the soul does not depart immediately. It still feels close to the body. Jewish mysticism compares body and soul to a loving husband and wife. When a husband departs this world, can a loving wife immediately move on? The bond is so close that time is needed to adjust to the new reality.

The soul, then, does not abandon the body immediately after death. Since it is confused and disoriented, it stays close to what it knows best — its body. It hovers around the body until burial, and shares in the mourning during shivah, going back and forth from gravesite to the shivah house.[197]

---

196 See Rabbi Bachya ibn Paquda, "Shaar HaBechinah," in *Duties of the Heart*, trans. Daniel Haberman (New York: Feldheim Publishers, 1996), chapter 3, for more on the subject.

197 *Zohar* 1:122b. Based on Kabbalistic sources, the *Gesher HaChaim* (1:117) outlines seven stages of departure: (1) Thirty days before death, the soul begins a partial separation from the body. (2) In the last hours before death, there is a further separation. (3) At the moment of death, the soul leaves the body and meets its Maker. (4) For the first three days after death, the soul is confused. It believes it will reenter the body and

The soul is fully aware of what is happening.[198] One way to understand this soul-knowledge is to consider that upon its departure from the physical world, the soul achieves greater closeness and knowledge of God, Who is the Source of all knowledge, and thus the soul shares in God's knowledge of what is happening to its body on earth.

Comforting the Soul

Two common trends exist in the Western funeral industry. Some try to preserve the body as long as possible through embalming, metal caskets, sealed concrete vaults, and mausoleums. The other trend is the opposite — to burn the body immediately.

From a traditional Jewish perspective, both of these choices are painful to the soul. The soul has just left its home, the body. It is confused and needs to acclimate to a new disembodied reality. Allowing the body to gradually return to its roots allows a slow but steady adjustment to occur. Cremation deprives the soul of its ability to acclimate. Embalming prevents the soul's smooth transition to the next world. Both options cause the soul significant disorientation and anguish.

The goal of Jewish burial practices is not simply to comfort the mourner, as important as that is. Even when there are no mourners, and no one will sit shivah, Jewish burial practices do not change. The Talmud explains that while mourning practices are

---

therefore stays closely attached to it. After three days it ceases trying to reenter the body, but remains confused. During the shivah, the first week after death, the soul goes back and forth from the grave to the shivah house. (5) Between shivah and thirty days, the soul rises in Heaven, but is closely attached to the gravesite. (6) Between thirty days and the first year, the soul rises higher in Heaven, but still returns periodically to the gravesite. (7) After one year, it stays in Heaven, except for a small part of it that remains connected to this world and its body.

198 Talmud, Tractate *Berachot* 18b; *Tosafot, Shabbat* 153a, s.v. "*venishmato*"; Talmud, Tractate *Sotah* 34b; Rabbi Aaron Berachyah, *Ma'avar Yabok* 2:25; and Menashe ben Yisrael, *Nishmat Chaim* 2:22.

largely for the mourners, burial itself is *not* for the living — it is for the dead, enabling the soul to slowly disengage from its body.[199] The laws and customs of burial are designed to reflect the situation of the soul and to help it make a smooth transition to the next world. This is why traditional Jewish funeral practices are marked by tremendous respect for the body — it is painful for a soul to see its body mishandled, abandoned, or defiled.

A brochure from the National Association of Chevra Kadishas (NASCK) summarizes this well:

> When a person dies, the soul or neshama hovers around the body. This neshama is the essence of the person, the consciousness and totality. Its thoughts, deeds, experiences and relationships. The body was its container, while it lasted, and the neshama, now on the way to the Eternal World, refuses to leave until the body is buried. In effect, the totality of the person who died continues to exist for a while in the vicinity of the body. A Jewish funeral is therefore most concerned with the feelings of the deceased, not only the feelings of the mourners. How we treat the body and how we behave around the body must reflect how we would act around the very person himself at this crucial moment.[200]

---

199 Jerusalem Talmud, *Moed Katan* 3:5.
200 Rabbi Elchonon Zohn, *Dignity for the Body, Peace for the Soul: An Introduction to Jewish Burial Customs* (Richmond Hill, NY, 1994), http://www.shared.nasck.org/jewish_burial.pdf#zoom=75.

-17-
A Rational View of Resurrection

> It is no more surprising to be born twice than once;
> Everything in nature is resurrection.
> — Voltaire[201]

Modern people are open to believing in an afterlife. After all, we sense there is something more to life and trust that there must be — and is — some Heaven somewhere where everything will make sense and be good.

Modern people are also open to believing in reincarnation. While the concept seems strange at first, we do acknowledge the

---

[201] Consider also: "Nations, like stars, are entitled to eclipse. All is well, provided the light returns and the eclipse does not become endless night. Dawn and resurrection are synonymous. The reappearance of the light is the same as the survival of the soul" (Victor Hugo, *Les Miserables*), and "Every parting gives a foretaste of death; every coming together again a foretaste of the resurrection" (Arthur Schopenhauer, *The Essays of Arthur Schopenhauer: Studies in Pessimism*).

existence of a soul, and it is not that far-fetched to believe that a soul could return to earth at different times. Enough science fiction and New Age accounts have sensitized us to this idea.

Resurrection, though, is a different matter. Modern, rational people have trouble buying into the concept of resurrection. It seems like a ridiculous notion, bereft of any critical thought, and reserved for ultrareligious believers. Horror movies (and, perhaps, Michael Jackson's *Thriller* music video) associate the concept with evil skeletal figures rising from their graves in tattered clothing to attack the living. Intelligent people are supposed to believe in *that*?

On a deeper note, we wonder, "Why would God want resurrection anyway? When the body dies, shouldn't the soul just move on to a better place?"

Judaism places great importance on resurrection.[202] Our tradition directly and indirectly refers to the concept often, it is central to our prayers,[203] and Maimonides actually lists belief in resurrection as one of the thirteen principles of the Jewish faith:

> I believe with complete faith that there will be a revival of the dead at the time when it shall please the Creator, Blessed be His name ...[204]

---

202 Talmud, Tractate *Sanhedrin* 90b–91b. Note that several actual incidences of resurrection are recorded in the Bible: The prophet Elijah raises a young boy from death (1 Kings 17:17–24); Elisha raises the son of the Shunammite woman (2 Kings 4:32–37); and a dead man's body that was thrown into Elisha's tomb is resurrected when the body touches Elisha's bones (ibid. 13:21). The resurrection we refer to here, though, is the general resurrection of the dead that will take place sometime in the future. Some verses referring to this type of resurrection include: "Your dead will live; their corpses will rise. You who lie in the dust, awake and shout for joy, for your dew is as the dew of the dawn, and the earth will give birth to the departed spirits" (Isaiah 26:19); and when an angel tells the prophet Daniel, "Many of those who sleep in the dust of the ground will awake, some of these to everlasting life, but the others to disgrace and everlasting contempt" (Daniel 12:2).

203 For example, the second paragraph of the central *Amidah* prayer, which is recited a minimum of three times a day, every day of the year, focuses on it.

204 His original formulation doesn't include the words "I believe" with each principle, rather a description of each one. Tradition has used this formulation. See Mai-

How can we make sense of an idea that seems so foreign?

Jurassic Park

Resurrection in Jewish thought is quite different from what is portrayed in horror movies. The dead will not come back to attack us. Their "return" is a happy occasion, not a scary one.

How is resurrection possible?

The movie *Jurassic Park* may help. The premise of the movie is that millions of years ago, when insects would bite or sting a dinosaur, blood would then enter the insect, which would then get encased inside amber, which could survive until today.

In the film, scientists had developed a means of retrieving the DNA from the amber and "bringing the dinosaurs back to life." While currently impossible, the idea of bringing something back to life using DNA[205] is not as far-fetched as it once was. We can already use DNA to clone animals, so how different is DNA resurrection, after all?

The Talmud explains the concept thus: I didn't always exist. You didn't always exist. The world (according to Judaism and the big bang theory) didn't always exist. Matter didn't always exist. All of it was created, ex nihilo — from nothing. If something that never existed can come to exist, certainly something that already existed, and then ceased to be, can come back into existence.

In other words, God is the Giver of life. He creates a soul, a purely spiritual entity, and places it in a body in order to enable the soul to fulfill its mission in life. When that body is gone, God can certainly recreate the same body and place the soul within it once again.

---

monides' *Commentary to the Mishnah, Sanhedrin* 10:1. The thirteen principles are listed in many prayer books after the text of the morning services.

205 Jewish tradition (see *Sefer Ta'amei Haminhagim* 425 and *Bereishit Rabbah* 28:3) teaches that there is a minuscule bone called the *luz* bone, almost indestructible, which will be the source from which life is regenerated.

On a physical level, with modern technology, we can begin to see how the body could indeed be regenerated. Spiritually, too, we can comprehend how God places souls into bodies.

The main trouble we have with resurrection is not the *how* — that's believable enough (once given proper thought) — but the *why*? Why would God let someone die just to bring him back? And why should the body exist in the afterlife — isn't Heaven the place for souls?

The Body as Enemy

Many religions and philosophies understand life to be full of suffering, temptation, and sin. The body is, essentially, a trap. Give in to the body and sacrifice your soul. Choose your soul by sacrificing your body.

This dichotomy explains the celibacy of these religions' leaders and practitioners, and their encouragement of an ascetic lifestyle. The body, after all, is evil, and evil must be denied. It is not surprising, then, in this understanding, to note the absence of the body in the afterlife. *This world* contains physicality and its attendant evil. *That world*, beautiful and spiritual, should have no physicality at all.[206]

The Body as Partner

The Jewish tradition fundamentally disagrees with this view of the body and, therefore, with its corresponding view of the afterlife.

Physicality is indeed challenging: Will a man cheat on his wife for bodily pleasure, or remain loyal because it is the right thing to do?

---

[206] It is fitting that Hindus and ancient Greek philosophers both regarded the body as prison — and favored cremation instead of burial.

The body is not the enemy, however, as we have mentioned. We could not pray without our mouths. We could not give charity without our hands. We could not help an elderly person across the street without our legs. The body is the soul's partner in doing good and in bringing spirituality into daily life. The soul could not exist in this world without it. Physicality in the Jewish worldview is not meant to be defeated — it is meant to be elevated. This explains why activities such as delicious Shabbat and holiday meals are actually mitzvot, commandments. The body is the soul's partner, not its enemy.

Our bodies *help* our spiritual development. And, since the body helps earn reward in this world, it also deserves to receive reward in the afterlife.

Put another way, the point of life is to improve. To change. To rise from the mundane and add meaning and spirituality into everyday life. The natural consequence of developing spirituality is that one will be able to better connect to God in the afterlife. One who appreciates music will enjoy a great symphony more than one who has never bothered developing this appreciation. One who appreciates spirituality will enjoy the pure spirituality of Heaven more than one who has no concept of spirituality. Since our bodies helped develop our spirituality along the way, they too became more spiritual and therefore will also enjoy the spirituality of the afterlife.

Judaism posits that body and soul are partners:

> The human body is the interface between spiritual soul and physical world. The soul without the body cannot interact with the world and so cannot fulfill its task. The body without the soul is simply matter, lacking free will and spirituality.[207]

---

207 Mordechai Becher, *Gateway to Judaism* (New York: Mesorah Publications, 2005), 60.

God Himself chose to put this body and soul together because they are a perfect match. They are partners throughout life, becoming (very) attached to each other. And they continue to be partners after death, via bodily resurrection.

Resurrection is, then, simply a fancy way of saying that physicality can indeed be spiritual, and that, by definition, all spirituality lives forever.

Life Matters

One approach to the afterlife is that the spirit lives on without the body. We have seen how this approach is based on denying the body rather than appreciating and elevating it. Another problem with this approach is that on a deep level it seems to belittle human life. By denying the importance of the body after death, it also subtly downplays the importance of the body while alive. After all, physicality is, in the grand scheme of things, very temporary and inconsequential.

So, in this bodiless approach to eternity, does physical life today really matter? If physical reality is only a façade, a temporary struggle against the body, how important can *your* physical life be? How important is anything that happens in the world? No wonder that many influenced by this doctrine do not struggle against death, but rather accept it for themselves … and others.

Resurrection teaches us how much our physical life matters. As the renowned sociologist of religion Will Herberg put it:

> [The] whole point of the doctrine of resurrection is that the life we live now, the life of the body, the life of empirical existence in society, has some permanent

worth in the eyes of God and will not vanish in the transmutation of things at the "last day."[208]

Resurrection teaches that our bodies matter. That what we do with our physical lives matters. That how we act matters.

Resurrection teaches that not only do our souls live forever, but our actions do as well.

Resurrection implies that individuals matter (for each of us will return as individuals) and that community matters (for we will be brought back together).

Resurrection teaches that our lives, here on the planet we experience and know, matter.

God's Involvement

Those who believe in a purely spiritual afterlife without bodily resurrection seem to suggest that the soul is immortal, and that its eternality is independent and automatic. In other words, the soul survives after death occurs … because souls are eternal and that is what they do. The soul never actually died. The body died. Souls don't die.

Notice that God seems to be left out of this process. Lip service may be paid to His creating the system, but it pretty much runs itself afterwards.

Resurrection, on the other hand, includes death and rebirth. Examples often given of resurrections or resurrection-like experiences are flowers blossoming in the spring after a frozen, dead winter, or a person waking up after sleep. Resurrection is *not* automatic. There was death — not just a shedding of a temporary physical body — and God gives life, once again. Resurrection is

---

[208] Will Herberg, *Judaism and the Modern Man: An Interpretation of Jewish Religion* (New York: Farrar, Straus and Young, 1951), 229.

a classic tenet of monotheism because of the necessary active involvement of God.

God's Triumph

Implicit in resurrection is the idea that God wins.

Death, the end of His most precious creation — life — seems problematic for God. In the Bible, death only occurs after Adam and Eve sin and eat from the forbidden tree. Death is the result of failure. If material reality disappears, it is as if God's world simply is not worthy of eternity and cannot enter the "big leagues." Like the skin of a snake that is shed, physicality is forgotten.

Resurrection declares that *all* of God's creations — physical and spiritual — can, in some way, merit eternal life. God's power is not limited in any way, for even the bodies He creates are unlimited in their potential. God can make physicality eternal. God triumphs over death.

Cremation and Resurrection

Resurrection is fundamental to Jewish thought and tradition.

That same Jewish tradition sees cremation as a rejection of the concept of resurrection.[209]

Why? Can't God resurrect a body from cremated ashes?

Of course He can. Monotheism is predicated on God's Omnipotence — He can do anything.[210] Nevertheless, by willfully and unnecessarily burning the body, cremation works against resurrection

---

209 Rabbi Chaim Ozer Grodzinsky, *Achiezer* 3:72; *Beit Yitzchak, Yoreh Dei'ah* 2:155. See also Talmud, Tractate *Gittin* 56b.
210 And I have no doubts that He will mercifully fix the ashes of unwilling victims of cremation such as those who were murdered in the Nazi ovens. As Rabbi Elchonon Zohn, foremost authority on burial issues in the United States and the head of the Chevra Kadisha of Queens, New York, pointed out to me upon reviewing this manuscript, the Talmud (Tractate *Gittin* 57b, see *Maharsha* and others) indicates clearly

and implies a rejection of God's creation and commandments. God emphasized that He values the body and wants it treated with reverence. He attaches such importance to it that He intends to ultimately bring it back. Cremation implicitly denies or minimizes all of this.

Burial, on the other hand, accepts God's teachings of the importance of our physical lives — and affirms His plan for the future. Burial emphasizes the inherent sanctity of our physical bodies — and teaches us to care for them, both before and after death.

---

that those whose bodies are destroyed against their will (*al kiddush Hashem* — in sanctification of God's Name) will indeed be resurrected.

Summary of Part 4

- During a lifetime together, a soul becomes very attached to its body, like husband and wife. Upon death, the soul does not leave its body immediately.

- As the soul leaves its body and gets closer to God, its understanding of the world increases. It is aware of what is happening to its body.

- While many mourning practices exist to comfort the mourner, the burial itself is primarily for the soul, to escort it properly into its next stage.

- Cremation creates great pain and anguish for the departed soul and hinders it from returning to God.

- While resurrection seems strange to contemporary ears, as Voltaire put it, "It is no more surprising to be born twice than once." Scientifically, the idea of using DNA to regenerate life is not as far-fetched as it once was.

- Resurrection is core part of classic Judaism. It teaches that our bodies matter. That what we do with our physical lives matters. That how we act matters.

- Resurrection teaches not only that our souls live forever, but that our actions do as well.

- Judaism considers cremation to be a rejection of resurrection. While God can indeed do anything, choosing cremation shows opposition to God's commandments, plan, and wishes.

Conclusion

Cremation is becoming more and more acceptable in the Western world. It seems cheaper than burial, simpler, and better for the environment. But the reality is otherwise.

Cremation expenses can be considerable, and are often the same as the cost of burials. Even when cremation is cheaper (i.e., when direct cremation is chosen, with no services of any kind), nevertheless there are crucial reasons to choose burial.

Cremation is neither quick nor clean. A long, gruesome process takes place behind the incinerator's doors, even worse than natural decomposition in the ground — which is, after all, the way of all living beings.

In our mobile world, children often live in different cities than their parents do, making cemetery visitation harder. But burial is important with or without visitation, and cremation doesn't even solve mobility problems: Unwanted urns pile up and are eventually discarded. The body is not given a permanent home.

Despite the publicity of the cremation industry, environmentalists are actually *against* cremation due its high use of fossil fuels and toxic emissions.

Choosing burial is more significant than many realize. It represents and reinforces how we view life. Burial emphasizes the dignity and worth of human life and how our actions — done with our physical bodies — have eternal value. Cremation, on the other hand, destroys the body, symbolizing and promoting the marginalization of the worth of physical life, and of the individual.

Burial is a clear and strong requirement of Judaism. For thousands of years, no matter the changing customs and preferences of our surrounding societies, we have stuck to our tradition and made enormous efforts to provide proper burials for all, whether rich or poor.

Jews have always understood that there is much we don't understand. There are coincidences we can't explain, and deep meaning that we only sense in the quiet moments. There is an eternal spirit that lives on after physical death. Jewish mystical sources teach that this spirit — the soul — of the recently departed is troubled by cremation, which causes it great pain and hinders its ability to naturally transition to the next world.

Choosing burial is the right Jewish choice. Cremation is the antithesis of Jewish tradition, law, and philosophy, while burial fulfills a religious commandment. Furthermore, it connects us with our ancestors, who, for thousands of years, made proper Jewish burial a high priority. Choosing burial also declares that the forced cremations of the victims of the Holocaust were an unforgivable attempt to destroy the identity of millions of Jews, declaring that they — and thus we — had never existed.

I'm Jewish

On January 23, 2002, Jewish American journalist Daniel Pearl, bureau chief for the Wall Street Journal, was kidnapped by Al-Qaeda in Pakistan.

He was tortured and, nine days later, on February 1, 2002, beheaded.

Shortly thereafter a video was released by the kidnappers. Some of his last words included:

"My name is Daniel Pearl.

"I am a Jewish American from Encino, California, USA …

"My father's Jewish, my mother's Jewish, I'm Jewish."

These words inspired Jews around the world. Schoolchildren studied them. Books were written about them. Organizations were created to spread their message.

Why the reaction? People understood that although he was in dire circumstances, Pearl did not denounce his heritage or avoid it. Rather, he declared his Jewish pride: "I'm Jewish."

In our own way, without the tragedy of terrorism, each of us can do the same. Cremation may be in style now. That may last a year, a decade, or a century. Things change. No matter what others do, though, by choosing burial we can make a final declaration:

> While I wasn't perfect, I am a Jew and happy to be one.
> In this, my last act on Planet Earth, I want to be buried as a Jew — and state clearly and proudly, "I'm Jewish."

- Appendix A -
An Introduction to Jewish Burial Customs[211]

by Rabbi Elchonon Zohn

The Soul Is Present

When a person dies, the soul (in Hebrew, *neshamah*) hovers around the body. The soul is the essence of the person, its consciousness and the totality of its thoughts, deeds, experiences, and relationships. The body was its container and its partner in this world. The soul, on its way to the Eternal World, refuses to leave until the body is buried, and continues to exist for awhile in the vicinity of the body.

Jewish funeral and mourning practices are therefore extremely concerned with the feelings of the deceased, not only the feelings of the mourners. How we treat the body and how we behave around it must reflect how we would act around the very soul itself at this sensitive time. Now more than ever, the body deserves re-

---

211 Adapted with permission from *Dignity for the Body, Peace for the Soul: An Introduction to Jewish Burial Customs*, available in full at http://www.shared.nasck.org/jewish_burial.pdf#zoom=75.

spect — for the soul of the departed is very aware of what happens to its body.

Since leaving the body unattended would imply a certain amount of disregard, we arrange for a *shomer* (guard) to be present. These guards stay with the body day and night, reciting passages from the Book of Psalms, lending great comfort to the soul while it waits for its body's burial and its own ascent to the Eternal World.

Taharah — Washing

A newborn is immediately cleaned and washed when it enters the world. So, too, when a person leaves this world and prepares for "rebirth" in a new spiritual world, a *taharah* (ritual cleansing) is performed by members of the *chevra kadisha* (burial society). This is a sensitive and complete cleansing and dressing of the body, performed according to Jewish law and ancient custom. Prayers asking for the forgiveness of the deceased and the soul's eternal peace are offered. While taharah requires that the body be made as presentable as possible, nevertheless embalming, applying cosmetics, or any other attempts to create a lifelike appearance through artificial means are contrary to Jewish tradition and law.

Shrouds

The soul is about to face its judgment. Possessions and clothes don't matter — good deeds do. That's why every Jew is buried exactly alike, in a handmade, simple, clean white linen shroud that includes a white linen hat, shirt, pants, shoes, coat, and belt. The shrouds have no pockets to accentuate the fact that no worldly belongings accompany us. They are modeled after the white uniform worn by the high priest in the Holy Temple on Yom Kippur when he stood before God asking for the needs of his family and the entire Jewish people. These shrouds are therefore especially appropriate because soon after death, each and every soul asks for the needs of his or her family.

The Casket

"For dust you are and to dust you shall return."[212] This Biblical teaching guides us in selecting a casket. The casket must not be made of a material that slows down the body's natural return to nature. Wood is the only material allowed, and several holes are opened at the bottom to hasten the body's return to the earth. When vaults are required, they too should be open at the bottom. Viewing the body is seen as disrespectful to the memory of the deceased.

In-Ground Burial

The soul's return to heaven is dependent upon the body's return to the ground (as Ecclesiastes 12:7 says, "The dust returns to the earth … and the spirit returns to God who gave it"). Jewish law is therefore concerned with the immediacy of burial and the natural decomposition of the body. Mausoleums are forbidden since they retard the process of return to the earth. Cremation is certainly forbidden. Burial is directly into the ground, with family members and friends helping to fill the grave completely until a mound is formed. We make no attempt to retard the body's decomposition.

The Role of the Chevra Kadisha

Preparing the deceased for burial is an especially great mitzvah (commandment or good deed). Throughout Jewish history, therefore, being a member of the chevra kadisha has been a great honor.

---

212 Genesis 3:19.

Members of the burial society are selected for their character, integrity, and personal devotion to Jewish tradition. These men and women are constantly on call to perform a taharah and to ensure that Jewish burials are executed properly. Their greatest concern is the sensitive care, modesty, and dignity of the deceased. Men care for men, women care for women — and Jews care for fellow Jews. There is no better way to ensure the dignity of the body than to entrust its preparation to the chevra kadisha.

- Appendix B -
An Introduction to Jewish Mourning Customs[213]

by Lori Palatnik

Judaism provides a beautiful, structured approach to mourning that involves three stages. When followed carefully, these stages guide mourners through the tragic loss and pain and gradually ease them back into the world. One mourner said her journey through the stages of mourning was like being in a cocoon. At first she felt numb and not perceptively alive, yet gradually she emerged as a butterfly ready again to fly.

Stage One: Shivah

Immediately upon returning from the cemetery after the burial, and before entering the "shivah house" (explained below), mourners and anyone else who attended the burial perform a cer-

---

213 Adapted with permission from Lori Palatnik's *Remember My Soul: What to Do in Memory of a Loved One* (New York: Khal Press, 2008).

emonial washing of the hands. Mourners then partake in a "meal of condolence" provided by neighbors or the community, showing support and love.

Mourners then begin a seven-day period of intense mourning (*shivah* is from the word *sheva*, which means "seven"). This week is called "sitting shivah," and is an emotionally and spiritually healing time where the mourners sit low and dwell together, and friends and loved ones come to comfort them with short visits referred to as "shivah calls." A person sits shivah after having lost a parent, spouse, sibling, or child.[214] During shivah, we de-emphasize our own physicality by not pampering our bodies, in order to remind ourselves that what we are missing at this time is not the physical person who is gone, but the essence of who that person was — his or her soul.

A shivah house requires low chairs for mourners to sit on and memorial candles. Mirrors should be covered. Physical relations between a husband and wife are suspended during the week of shivah. A mourner should wear either stocking feet or slippers not made of leather — symbolizing the disregard for vanity and physical comfort.

One who is mourning should also refrain from bathing or showering for pleasure (one can do so for cleanliness), wearing makeup and anointing (with creams or perfume), getting a haircut (applies for the first thirty days), nail trimming, wearing freshly laundered garments for pleasure (can be worn for cleanliness), wearing new clothes, and washing clothes.

When one pays a shivah call, the focus is on comforting the mourners in their time of greatest grief. Traditionally, one enters the shivah house quietly with a small knock so as not to startle those inside. Mourners are not hosts: they do not greet visitors, serve them, or see them out. One who has come to comfort mourners should not greet them. Come in quietly, sit down close

---

214 Other loved ones are also mourned, but the observances of shivah do not apply.

to them, and take your cue from them. If they feel like speaking, let them indicate it to you by speaking first. If they are comfortable doing so, it is best to speak about the one who has passed away, and if you have any stories or memories to share with the mourner, this is the time to do so.

This is not a time to distract mourners from mourning. If the mourners do not feel like talking at that time, so be it. Your goal is not to get them to talk — it is to comfort them and your presence alone is doing that. By sitting there silently, you are saying more than words can. You are saying: "I am here for you. I feel your pain. There are no words."

Prayer services are held in the shivah house, not in the synagogue. Kaddish is recited. A traditional statement of comfort is said to the mourners just before leaving the shivah house. It can be said in either Hebrew or English:

> May God comfort you among the other mourners of Zion and Jerusalem.
> *Ha-Makom y'nachem et'chem b'toch sha'ar aveilei Tzion v'Yerushalayim.*

The mourner should nod or say "Amen," and you should quietly depart.

Stage Two: Shloshim

The first thirty days following the burial (which include the shivah) are called *shloshim*, from the word meaning "thirty." Most restrictions that applied to mourners during the seven-day shivah period are now lifted as they begin a gradual reentry into life. However, they should severely limit social engagements during this time, and certainly avoid festive outings where music is played. Mourners do not shave or cut their hair during this time.

For those mourning a spouse, a sibling, or a child, official mourning ends after shloshim — Kaddish is no longer recited and they can resume activities without restriction.

Stage Three: The One-Year Period

During the twelve-month period from the day of death, one who has lost a parent is still considered a mourner, for the loss of a parent requires a longer period of adjustment and reflection. Social engagements are allowed, but the pursuit of entertainment and amusement, especially where music is involved, is curtailed. One is allowed to actively engage in business activities. After the year is complete, one is not considered a mourner.

Other Remembrances

A short memorial service (called *Yizkor* or "remembrance") is held in the synagogue on the holidays of Yom Kippur, the last day of Passover, the last day of Shavuot, and the eighth day of Sukkot (Shemini Atzeret). After the holiday is complete, it is appropriate to give *tzedakah*, a charitable donation, in your loved one's memory.

Each year on the Jewish anniversary of the death[215] (the *yahrtzeit*) of a loved one, a proper commemoration should take place. If you are not sure of the Jewish date, contact a synagogue, yeshiva, or funeral home and they will surely help you. Some customs that people do on the yahrtzeit include: (a) lighting a yahrtzeit candle at home the night before, because the Jewish day begins in the evening; (b) giving tzedakah in your loved one's memory; (c) learn

---

215 Why does Judaism emphasize the date of death rather than the birthday? The Talmud compares this to a ship. How odd that we hold a big party when the ship is about to sail, yet when it arrives at its destination, nothing is done. It really should be the other way around. Although the day of birth holds all the potential for the life that will be, the day of death is the marker of who we actually became, the good things we accomplished, and the positive ways we lived up to our potential.

Torah that day — read from a book about Judaism or Torah ideas, or arrange to learn with someone from the community; (d) recite Kaddish, or, if you cannot, arrange for someone to recite it on your behalf; (e) sponsor a kiddush in synagogue on that day, or on the Shabbat that falls at the end of that week.

The tombstone gives honor to the body that housed the soul. The tombstone is usually set up sometime between the shivah and the first yahrtzeit. Recently the ceremony (*hakamat matzeivah* — raising up the stone) has been referred to as an "unveiling." Those close to the family are invited to the gravesite, where the mourners unveil the stone covered by a cloth. The ceremony is usually short. Psalms are recited, and people often share thoughts about the deceased.

Although a person can visit the cemetery at any time, there are special days for visiting the grave that are particularly conducive to reflection: (a) the seventh day, after ending the restrictions of shivah; (b) the shloshim, the thirtieth day of mourning; (c) the completion of the first twelve months of mourning; (d) the yahrtzeit, the anniversary of the death, every year; (e) the day before Rosh Hashana; (f) the day before Yom Kippur.

The Jewish custom is not to bring flowers to the graves, but instead to place a simple stone on the gravestone itself. Rather than spend money on flowers which quickly die, it is better to give money in the person's memory to tzedakah, which helps to elevate the person's soul.

Final Thoughts

The process of mourning is not easy, and the Jewish tradition provides a structure to let mourners feel their aloneness, separating them from the outside world and then gradually reinstating them back into society. The different stages of mourning allow us to come to grips with the loss. While the loss is forever, the psychological, emotional, and spiritual healing that takes place at each of these stages is necessary and healthy.

May the Almighty comfort all the mourners of Zion and Jerusalem.

- Appendix C -
Cremation in Israel?[216]

by Rabbi Avi Shafran

A crematorium recently opened for business in the Israeli town of Hadera, for the use of citizens who want their remains reduced to ashes.

A decade ago, 20 percent of Americans who died were cremated. In 2005, the rate had risen to 32 percent. The Cremation Association of North America confidently forecasts that by 2025 more than half of Americans will choose to have their remains burned rather than interred. While no one knows what percentage of American cremation choosers are Jewish, there is little doubt that, at least among Jews with limited or no Jewish education, or who became estranged from Jewish observance, cremation has become acceptable, if not a vogue. And now, the Jewish state has its own facility for burning human bodies.

---

216 Reproduced with author's permission from "Burning Issue: The Jewish State Gets Its First Crematorium — Why It Matters," *Jewish World Review,* February 5, 2007, http://www.jewishworldreview.com/avi/shafran_cremation.php3.

Yet the fact that the establishment is the first of its kind in Israel does bespeak an essential Jewish attitude toward the services it provides.

Some Jews recoil from the idea of cremation because the Third Reich incinerated so many of its Jewish victims.

Others, and many non-Jews, disdain the burning of human remains because of infamous cases where crematory owners, after accepting families' payments, presented them with urns of animal ashes, turning a further profit from the sale of the bodies entrusted them to brokers who then conducted brisk businesses of their own selling body parts.

Judaism's inherent abhorrence for cremation, however, predates and supersedes both Nazi evils and ghoulish crimes. The roots of the Torah's insistence on burial of human remains lie elsewhere.

Judaism's opposition to cremation is sourced in the Torah's statement that humans are created "in the image of God." As a result, we are charged to show "honor for the dead" by consigning human bodies, in as undisturbed state as possible, to the earth — even, if necessary, if it means forfeiting the performance of another commandment.

And then there is the related, fundamental Jewish belief that there will come a time when the dead will live again. Although the idea of the resurrection of the righteous may be surprising to some, it is one of Judaism's most important teachings. The concept, the Talmud teaches, is subtly evident in the written Torah's text; and fully prominent in the Torah's other half, the oral tradition. The Mishnah, the oral tradition's central text, confers such weightiness to the conviction that it places deniers of the eventual resurrection of the dead first among those who "forfeit their share in the world to come" (*Sanhedrin* 11:1). As the Talmud comments thereon: "He denied the resurrection of the dead, so will he be denied a portion in the resurrection of the dead."

That our bodies are invested with such importance should not be startling. Not only our souls but our physical selves, too, possess inherent holiness. Our bodies, after all, are the indispensable means of performing God's will. It is through employing them to do good deeds and denying their gravitations to sin that we achieve our purposes in this world.

And so, Jewish tradition teaches, even though we are to consign our bodies to the earth after death, there is a small "bone" (*etzem*) that is not destroyed when a body decays and from which the entire person, if he or she so merits, will be rejuvenated at some point in the future.

The idea that a person might be recreated from something tiny — something, even, that can survive for millennia — should not shock anyone remotely familiar with contemporary science. Each of our cells contains a large and complex molecule, DNA, that is essentially a blueprint of our bodies; theoretically, one of those molecules from even our long-buried remains could be coaxed to reproduce each of our physical selves. (*Etzem* can mean not only "bone" but also "essence" and "self.")

Burning, in Judaism, is a declaration of utter abandon and nullification. Jews burn leaven and bread before Passover, when the Torah insists no vestige of such material may be in their possession. The proper means of disposing of an idol is to pulverize or burn it.

Needless to say, God is capable of bringing even ashes to life again (as the ashes of the Nazis' crematoria victims will surely demonstrate one day, may it come soon). But actually choosing to have one's body incinerated is an act that, so intended or not, expresses denial of the fact that the body is still valuable, that it retains worth, indeed potential life.

The new Israeli crematorium's owner, in fact, describes himself as an atheist, as do most, if not all, of his customers. One, a teacher in Jerusalem, gave eloquent expression to her reasons for choosing cremation, telling the *Jerusalem Post*: "I was not sanctified in my lifetime so my grave won't be sanctified either … I believe that there is nothing after death …"

That is the philosophy underlying the choice of cremation.

It is the antithesis of the belief system called Judaism.

Selected Bibliography

Action Pennsylvania. "Crematoria." EJnet.org: Web Resources for Environmental Activists, April 20, 2009. http://www.ejnet.org/crematoria.

B & L Cremation Systems, Inc. "Crematory & Incinerator Frequently Asked Questions." B & L Cremation Systems. http://www.blcremationsystems.com/FAQCremation.html.

Balilty, Dan. "Israel's Agonizing Debate over Prisoner Swaps." *CBC News*, July 16, 2008. http://www.cbc.ca/world/story/2008/07/09/f-prisoner-swaps.html.

Begoun, Rabbi David. "Journey of the Soul: Cremation versus Burial." http://www.judaismwithoutwalls.org/audio.htm.

Bottum, Joseph. "Death & Politics." *First Things*, July 2007. http://www.firstthings.com/article/2009/02/001-death--politics-29.

Butz, Bob. *Going Out Green: One Man's Adventure Planning His Own Natural Burial*. Traverse City, MI: Spirituality & Health Books, 2009.

Cannon, Florence. "Our Honored Dead." *Quartermaster Review*, May-June 1952. http://www.qmmuseum.lee.army.mil/mortuary/Honored_Dead.htm.

Cook, Emma. "Saying Goodbye Our Way." *Guardian*, August 19, 2006. http://www.guardian.co.uk/lifeandstyle/2006/aug/19/familyandrelationships.family.

Deslauriers, Marc. *Emission Inventory Guidebook.* Ottawa, ON: Environment Canada, Criteria Air Contaminants Division, 2006.

Diffen: Compare Anything. "Burial vs. Cremation." Diffen.com. http://www.diffen.com/difference/Burial_vs_Cremation.

Dummer, T. J. B., H. O. Dickinson, and L. Parker. "Incinerators May Put Babies at Risk." *Journal of Epidemiology and Community Health* 57, May 29, 2003, 456–461.

Evans, W.E.D. *The Chemistry of Death.* Springfield, IL: Charles C. Thomas Publishers, 1963.

Green Cremations. www.green-cremations.com/Cremation%20Info.htm (accessed June 2010).

Harris, Mark. *Grave Matters: A Journey through the Modern Funeral Industry to a Natural Way of Burial.* New York: Scribner, 2007.

Howard, Donald. *Burial or Cremation: Does It Matter?* New York: Banner of Truth Press, 2001.

Iserson, Kenneth V. *Death to Dust: What Happens to Dead Bodies?* Tucson, AZ: Galen Press, 1999.

Kardares, Molly. "Another Sign of the Recession — Cremation on the Rise." *CBS News*, March 20, 2009. http://www.cbsnews.com/blogs/2009/03/20/business/econwatch/entry4879269.shtml.

Kendall, Dr. Perry. "Put a Lid on Fumes from Cremation." *Vancouver Sun*, May 12, 2006.

Kerrigan, Michael. *The History of Death: Burial Customs and Funeral Rites, from the Ancient World to Modern Times.* Guilford, CT: Lyons Press, 2007.

Selected Bibliography

Krishman, Sonia. "Thousands of Cremated Remains Go Unclaimed." *Seattle Times*, May 23, 2008. http://www.seattletimes.nwsource.com/html/localnews/2004433569_remains23m.html.

Lubowski, Ruben N., Marlow Vesterby, Shawn Bucholtz, Alba Baez, and Michael J. Roberts. *Major Uses of Land in the United States, 2002/EIB-14.* United States Department of Agriculture: Economic Research Service, May 2006, http://www.ers.usda.gov/publications/eib14/.

Lynch, Thomas. *The Undertaking: Life Studies from the Dismal Trade.* New York: W. W. Norton & Company, 1997.

Matthews, Sarah. "Cremation: Burn, Baby, Burn." Free Online Library, August 7, 2007. http://www.thefreelibrary.com/Cremation+Burn,+Baby,+Burn-a01073972282.

McAfee, Melonyce. "I'm Burning Up — How Much Will My Ashes Weigh?" *Slate Magazine*, July 26, 2006, http://www.slate.com/id/2146542/.

Memorial Society Fund. *How Much Will My Funeral Cost?* Hinesburg, VT: Funeral and Memorial Societies of America, Inc.

Moss, Rabbi Aaron. "Cremation: What Is the Jewish View?" *Jewish Magazine*, March 2007. http://www.jewishmag.com/112mag/cremation/cremation.htm.

National Funeral Directors Association. *Funeral Home Wastestream Audit Report.* National Funeral Directors Association, 1995.

New World Encyclopedia, s.v. "Cremation." http://www.newworldencyclopedia.org/entry/Cremation.

Novey, Joelle. "Greening Your Final Arrangements." *Green American,* July/August 2008. http://www.greenamerica.org/livinggreen/greenburial.cfm.

Paine, Thomas. *The Rights of Man.* Independence Hall Association in Philadelphia: USHistory.org. http://www.ushistory.org/paine/rights/c1-010.htm.

Palatnik, Lori, and Rabbi Yaakov Palatnik. *Remember My Soul: What to Do in Memory of a Loved One.* New York: Khal Press, 2008.

Pioneer Burials. http://www.pioneerburials.com/article_info.php?articles_id=2 (accessed September 1, 2009).

Promessa: Organic Burial. "Cremation." Promessa. http://www.promessa.se/facts/cremation/?lang=en.

Prothero, Stephen. *Purified by Fire: A History of Cremation in America.* Los Angeles: UCLA Press, 2001.

Rastogi, Nina. "The Green Hereafter: How to Leave an Environmentally Friendly Corpse." *Slate Magazine,* February 17, 2009. http://www.slate.com/id/2211395.

Reindl, John. *Summary of References on Mercury Emissions from Crematoria.* November 3, 2008. http://www.ejnet.org/crematoria/reindl.pdf.

Rosen, Fred. *Cremation in America.* Amherst, NY: Prometheus Books, 2004.

Roth, D.A. "Cremation: A Sometimes Difficult Subject." Casket-online.com. http://www.casket-online.com/Articles/031.cfm.

Rutherford, Richard. *Honoring the Dead: Catholics and Cremation Today.* Collegeville, MN: Liturgical Press, 2001.

Schmidt, Alvin. *Dust to Dust or Ashes to Ashes? A Biblical and Christian Examination of Cremation.* Salisbury, MA: Regina Orthodox Press, 2005.

Silverberg, Rabbi Naftali. "Why Does Jewish Law Forbid Cremation?" Chabad.org. http://www.chabad.org/library/article_cdo/aid/510874/jewish/Why-does-Jewish-law-forbid-cremation.htm.

Smith, Tom, and Tom Pfeifer. "Cremation and Creativity." *ICFM Magazine,* November 2005, http://www.iccfa.com/reading/2000-2009/cremation-and-creativity.

Spitz, Elie. "Why Bury?" in *Wrestling with the Angel.* Ed. Jack Riemer. New York: Schocken, 1995. 124–125.

State of California Department of Consumer Affairs: Cemetery and Funeral Bureau. *Consumer Guide to Funeral & Cemetery Purchases.* http://www.cfb.ca.gov/consumer/funeral.shtml.

Stevens, Hal. "Cremation or Burial — Carbon Emissions and the Environment." The Free Library, April 21, 2009, http://www.thefreelibrary.com/Cremation+or+Burial+-+Carbon+Emissions+and+the+Environment-a01073949157.

Tsai, Michelle. "Bar-B-You: What's the Smell of Burning Human Flesh?" *Slate Magazine,* March 26, 2007. http://www.slate.com/id/2162676/.

Tucazinsky, Rabbi Yechiel Michel. *Gesher HaChaim (The Bridge of Life).* New York: Moznaim, 1983.

Wikipedia, s.v. "Cremation." http://en.wikipedia.org/wiki/Cremation.

Willaeys, Veerle. *Public Health Impact of Crematoria.* Memorial Society of British Columbia. http://www.memorialsocietybc.org/c/g/cremation-report.html.

Zohn, Rabbi Elchonon. *Dignity for the Body, Peace for the Soul: An Introduction to Jewish Burial Customs.* Richmond Hill, NY: 1994.

About the Author

Doron Kornbluth is the best-selling author of *Why Be Jewish? Knowledge and Inspiration for Jews of Today* and *Raising Kids to LOVE Being Jewish* (both published by Mosaica Press). A world-renowned speaker, his interactive and engaging talks are popular around the world, and he lectures in over fifty cities a year. Doron is also a popular tour guide in Israel, inspiring first-time and veteran visitors of all ages and backgrounds. Sign-up for his free e-newsletter or contact him via his website, www.doronkornbluth.com.

In Memoriam

Hershel Haikins

of blessed memory

whose passing was on

December 8, 1989

and his loving wife

Rose Haikins

of blessed memory

whose passing was on

April 10, 1986

May their memory be perpetuated through the accomplishments of this book.

In Memoriam

Bernard Goldberg

of blessed memory

whose passing was on

February 19, 1986

and his loving wife

Miriam Goldberg

of blessed memory

whose passing was on

September 23, 1992

May their memory be perpetuated through the accomplishments of this book.

Dedicated to

My Dear Uncle

Arnold Ben Reuvain

May his soul be elevated in heaven.

My uncle was a very special person who helped many others throughout his life. Through the kindness of his family, the support of the community, and incredible miracles surrounding his passing, he merited a kosher Jewish burial and calmly returned his soul to his Creator.

May God bless his family with good health, good lives, eternal joy, and to "return unto the Lord our God and hearken to His voice."

Robin Davina Meyerson

Honoring the Deceased

For thousands of years, Jews have prayed, studied, and done good deeds in memory of their deceased loved ones, bringing merit to their souls and emphasizing the positive influence the deceased had on the living.

According to tradition, there are three main ways to honor the deceased:

- Saying Kaddish in synagogue daily for the first year after passing and on a yahrtzeit (anniversary of passing),
- Studying Mishnah, and
- Reciting the Yizkor prayer at the appropriate times.

Whenever possible, it is ideal for mourners themselves to take on these obligations. If you are able and willing to do these — wonderful! Contact us if you need help figuring out what to do and when.

However, in today's busy world, many mourners cannot commit to "doing the right thing" on a regular basis for their loved ones, as much as they'd like to. In cases like these, we can help arrange for the prayers, study, and rituals to be performed on your behalf in memory of the dearly departed. We are honored to help you honor the memory of your loved one, in whatever way(s) you decide.

Please visit us at:
JewishDeathAndMourning.org
Tel: 888-6-KADDISH (652-3347)
Fax: 732-520-6483

We were married 47 years and all that time he took care of me. Knowing that his soul is benefitting greatly from Torah study on his Yartzeit and that Kaddish is being said for him every year gives me great comfort. I know it makes a difference to his soul. That's why I use the services of Jewish Death And Mourning to benefit my dear departed husband.

Shirley M.
Boca Raton, Florida

"I miss my husband Harry so much"

Services we provide:
• KADDISH • YIZKOR • MISHNAH STUDY

888-6-KADDISH (888-652-3347) **JewishDeathAndMourning.org**

Keep Your Family Jewish with

Raising Kids to LOVE Being Jewish

Bestselling author and renowned speaker Doron Kornbluth has taught thousands of Jewish parents and grandparents how to keep their families Jewish. Now his time-tested positive approach is available in an easy-to-read and easier-to-do format, sharing principles and practical tips for families of all backgrounds and ages. A pleasure to read — and do!

They'll *want* to stay Jewish with

Why Be Jewish?

This inspiring collection of over twenty unique and personal perspectives focuses on the central question facing most Jewish people today: Why bother being Jewish, anyway? Based on true stories from around the world, these pieces are touching, thought-provoking, meaningful, and funny. Gain clarity and confidence in why you're Jewish.

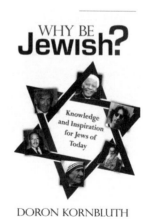

Available at bookstores everywhere or at www.mosaicapress.com

Dear Dad*

Dear Dad,

It's really hard for me to write this letter. I love you more than anything. You and Mom brought me into this world. You guided me and made me the strong, independent, thinking person I am. I have so many fond memories of my childhood with you — listening to classical music, swimming in the pool and laughing as you threw me up into the air, accompanying you to work and going to ball games...

I want to ask you something — something very important to me — but ultimately even more important to you. I don't know how to say this, since we never really have deep conversations. Of course, we talk, but it's mostly about the day-to-day stuff — not the really deep, meaningful stuff. So I just have to blurt it out:

Please arrange now that when the time comes, you'll have a traditional Jewish funeral and burial. There, I've said it and it's in

---

* This letter is adapted with permission from a sample letter written by Mrs. Robin Davina Meyerson.

writing. I don't want to be morbid, and of course I want you to live forever. But it's important that we talk about this openly now, before it's too late.

I know that you say you don't really believe in "all that religious Jewish stuff" and that once you're dead, you're dead, so nothing else matters. I know how you feel, but this is really important to me.

You raised me to be proud of being Jewish. I am. And, in my own way, I've been bringing more Jewish knowledge and practice into my life. Our wonderful tradition emphasizes over and over again how important proper Jewish burial is.

I want this for you. And I want this for me, and for my children — whom I hope also will be proud Jews and feel close to our heritage. I want to know it was handled correctly. I hope we can talk about it and that you'll come to feel the same way. But even if you don't, please give me one last gift — I am asking you with all my heart to clearly write down that when the time comes, I will be able to oversee all the details to ensure that you have a proper Jewish burial. I'm attaching a form** to make this easier for you to do.

You've given me so much. Even if you don't understand it, please grant me this request as well.

Do this for me. Do it for your grandchildren. Do it for yourself.

With more love and respect than you can imagine,
Your daughter

** Available at no charge from JewishDeathAndMourning.org.

Dear Son[*]

Dear Son,

I've told you how much I love you. I've shared my innermost dreams, thoughts, and hopes for you. And I've given you direction as to how to deal with all the financial and legal questions that will come before you after I am gone.

In this letter, I want to address something we once discussed, but not in enough detail: I am asking you, clearly, and without any ambiguity, to provide for me a fully traditional Jewish burial. The funeral director may be rushed and settle for something "kosher style." That is *not* what I want: I want a fully kosher burial, so I want to make it clear, in writing. I'm attaching an official form to that effect but want to write a more personal request and explanation here.

I want everything: The *chevra kadisha* (Jewish burial society) watching over my body and ritually washing it; a *shomer* (guard-

---

[*] The idea and format of this letter came from an anonymous "Dear Sean" letter circulating the Internet dealing with Jewish continuity.

ian) sitting with me and saying psalms until the actual burial; my body wrapped in shrouds or a tallis and placed in a simple pine box, covered with some of the dirt of the Holy Land; traditional prayers said. Also, I want some Hebrew on the tombstone. Include my Jewish name, Yaakov ben David, my Hebrew birth date, and my *yahrtzeit* (day of death).

You may be surprised at how important this is to me and that I am actually taking the time to write it out to you in detail. If you, God forbid, need to deal with this tomorrow, I'm sure that you'll do the right thing. However, I hope you won't have to deal with this request for many years to come and I want to make sure that no misunderstandings, forgetfulness, or haziness creep into the picture. Also, I want you to pass this letter on to other relatives so they will understand and, perhaps, think about what arrangements they want to make for themselves.

You know and I know that I wasn't the most religious person on the planet. But this is different. I know it is becoming more common, but when my time on the planet is over, *don't* cremate me. People claim that cremation is better for the environment. Poppycock. Burning anything is bad for the environment, son, including bodies. The cremation industry doesn't want you to think about the energy used and the pollutants released in the air. I want my body returning to Mother Earth and helping, in some small way, to replenish it, not pollute it.

People also claim that what happens to the body is not important. It is, after all, just a shell. The real "me" is the soul. Hard to argue with such an inspirational, loving image, except that … it's also poppycock. I'm not an Eastern mystic who believes we have no choice but to "suffer" through the physical world, and therefore spends his life celibate and ascetic on a mountaintop. I'm a Jew. And Judaism understands that the body is not evil. And it is not "just a shell." My body allowed me to speak, hear, smell, smile, see, walk, talk, run, give, touch … and produce you. My body allowed "me" to have a life. To interact. To struggle. To improve. I owe it a great deal. I don't want to burn it like the trash.

As to the claim that the land belongs to the living, well, you can guess what I think about that. How many racetracks do we need, after all? There is no shortage of land: next time you fly, note the massive amounts of empty, unused land in the world. There is plenty of land for the living and there always will be — and a dead person has a right to a small corner of the land saying, "I lived!" Besides, living people need the connection to the past that a cemetery provides, as well as its reminder of mortality. So don't buy into these pro-cremation arguments. They don't add up.

The truth is that fads come and go throughout history. When I was young, ties were thin. Then they got wide. Now they're becoming thin once again. Bell-bottoms were in, then out, then in again. Everything has its fads, even important issues like funerals and burials.

I don't want to be caught up in a fad. I want to die as a Jew. Jews have always — for over three thousand years — buried their loved ones in the traditional way. No embalming. No cremation. No shortcuts. I want to continue this chain.

I want to be buried as a Jew. True, I didn't choose to be a Jew, and I wasn't always the best one. But I've always felt that being Jewish was a gift. I didn't ignore it or rebel against it. I made it a central part of my identity. I gave you a Jewish education and sent you to Israel. I did my best so that you would, hopefully, feel the pride (and responsibility) in being Jewish.

I want to end my time on this funny planet on a good note. On the right note. To tell God, family, friends, and community that here lived a Jew. A proud one.

Will it cost more to bury? Probably. I've never had much money, you know. You never lacked for anything, but you also never had that much of anything (this latter point was as much a gift as the former, in my humble opinion, but you'll have to decide that for yourself). I have left you enough to cover the costs of a decent funeral. In the event that I need prolonged care and the money runs out, I ask you to still provide a fully kosher funeral. When you subtract the embalming (God forbid — don't let those modern mutilators touch one hair on my hairless head!) and fancy casket (against Jewish tradition anyway, as is embalming), there really isn't much of a difference. And the rabbi can probably arrange something kosher, respectful, and cheaper anyway.

Even if, for whatever reason, the burial ends up costing more, spend the money on me, son. I spent enough on you. It is my last wish.

With love and thanks in advance,
Dad